AF255651

God's Plan for You

God's Plan for You

BY

A. M. DEIGLORIAM

RESOURCE *Publications* · Eugene, Oregon

GOD'S PLAN FOR YOU

Resource Publications
An Imprint of Wipf and Stock Publishers
199 W. 8th Ave., Suite 3
Eugene, OR 97401

www.wipfandstock.com

PAPERBACK ISBN: 978-1-6667-6748-3
HARDCOVER ISBN: 978-1-6667-6749-0
EBOOK ISBN: 978-1-6667-6750-6

01/31/23

Dedicated to my loving wife of 50 years, my family,
and my many friends.

Contents

Introduction

THE WORLD WE LIVE on is composed of continents, mountains, forests, deserts, islands, oceans, lakes, rivers, and streams. It is estimated that there are over 5,000 ethnic groups that populate this world and speak an estimated 6,500 different languages. Many of these people are subject to severe weather (i.e., tornadoes, hurricanes, typhoons, earthquakes, fires) and freezing cold and extreme heat. These people are governed by many different types of governments (i.e., Democracies, Dictatorships, Monarchy, Oligarchy, Totalitarianism). Most of these people live in groups in the same country, community or village where they share the same language, food, values, cultural norms, dress, etc. The many differences between these people act both as a bond and as a reason for distrust and conflict. Many of the wars and battles that have been fought throughout history have been fought due to greed, envy, lack of understanding and lack of love for your neighbor.

In the beginning God created man with a soul. Genesis 2:7 reads, "And the Lord God formed man of the ground, and breathed into his nostrils the breath of life, and man became a living soul." From that point in time man had a soul that could be used to worship and praise God, to be nurtured and strengthened, or be contaminated with sin and may even be lost to evil.

After Jesus was crucified and rose from the grave, He appeared to ten of the disciples in a locked room. John 20:22 reads, "And when he had said this, He breathed on them and said, Receive the Holy Spirit." It is believed at this point the disciples remembered the promise made by Jesus that the Holy Spirit would be in communion with their souls.

Acts 2:1–3 reads, "And when the day of Pentecost was fully come, they were with one accord in one place. And suddenly there came a sound from heaven, a rushing mighty wind, and it filled all the house where they were sitting. And there appeared unto them cloven tongues like fire, and it sat upon each of them."

Both the Apostle John and the Apostle Luke wrote about the indwelling of the Holy Spirit into man's soul. The resurrection of Jesus left a massive vacuum that could only be filled by the Holy Spirit. The indwelling of the Holy Spirit into man's soul created a soul that was encouraged and convicted by the Holy Spirit. It is believed that Pentecost (indwelling of the Holy Spirit) occurred 50 days after the resurrection of Jesus. It is also believed that is in agreement with Jewish tradition that there were 50 days between the Passover and the deliverance of the Law by Moses at Mount Sinai.

There are three words in the Bible that are used to describe man's spiritual being. They are heart, soul, and spirit. It is believed the soul is the spiritual reflection of a man's entire life. The spirit is the breath of the Almighty that gives him understanding. And, the heart is the spiritual housing for all of man's intellectual reasoning, emotions and desires.

It is believed that the word heart is used in the Bible over 1,000 times. God promised Israel they would return from exile with a new heart and a new spirit.

Ezekiel 11:19 reads, "And I will give them one heart, and I will put a new spirit within you: and I will take the stony heart out of their flesh, and will give them a heart of flesh:"

God is a just God who did judge the Israelites for their moral failures and allowed them to be captured and exiled to Babylon. God is a just God who will discipline his people for their moral failures and will also provide a path for those who repent of their sin and become believers.

It is difficult to understand why the heart of man is so deceitful and treacherous. However, the fall of man had a tremendous impact on man to the point to where the basic foundations of man's character were infected by sin. Even those who have made a confession of faith and have received the Holy Spirit struggle with the deceitful heart.

Mark 7:21–23 reads, "For from within, out of the heart of men, proceed evil thoughts, adulteries, fornications, murders, Thefts, covetousness, wickedness, deceit, lasciviousness, an evil eye, blasphemy, pride, foolishness: All these evil things come from within, and defile the man."

Consequently, only God can break the shackles that bind man to his sins. The first step is for man to a make a confession of faith, confess his sins and place his trust in God's grace. This confession of faith guarantees salvation; is life changing and will have a profound effect on man's entire life. This first step can be very difficult for some people. Many have struggled for many years and have become very proud of their accomplishments in the face of many obstacles. In many cases people will refused to acknowledge there is a God because of a lack of a sense of anything spiritual in their lives. For these people taking the second step of changing their lives and living in God's plan is difficult. In many cases, these people have spent a lifetime justifying their sin.

Mark 10:17–21 reads, "And when he was gone forth into the way, there came one running, and kneeled to him, and asked him, Good Master, what shall I do that I may inherit eternal life? And Jesus said unto him, Why callest thou me good? there is none good but one, that is, God. Thou knowest the commandments, Do not commit adultery, Do not kill, Do not steal, Do not bear false witness, Defraud not, Honor thy father and mother. And he answered and said unto him, Master, all these have I observed from my youth. Then Jesus beholding him loved him, and said unto him, One thing thou lackest: go thy way, sell whatever hast, and give to the poor, and thou shalt have treasures in heaven: and come, take up the cross, and follow me."

The rich young ruler loved his possessions and could not give them up even for eternal life with Jesus. There are many that simply worship their possessions and have made a career out of accumulating as many things as possible. They are driven by greed and self and have no love for their fellow man. Other people are addicted to a life style that is based on sin.

Jesus made sanctification possible for the believer by offering his own blood.

Hebrews 10:15–18 reads, "Whereof the Holy Ghost also is a witness to us: for after that he had said before, This is the covenant that I will make with them after those days, saith the lord, I will put my laws into their hearts, and in their minds will I write them; And their sins and iniquities will I remember no more. Now where remission of these is, there is no more offering for sin."

We as Christians are directed by the Holy Spirit and are locked in battle with the flesh with its affections and lusts. The Holy Spirit communes with the believer's spirit within his soul. This is a lifelong confrontation that demands that the believer grows with each challenge. Unfortunately, there are those like the rich young ruler who cannot change their life and cannot break the chains that tie them to a life of sin.

Galatians 5:22–25 reads, "But the fruit of the Spirit is love, joy, peace, longsuffering, gentleness, goodness, faith, Meekness, temperance: against such there is no law. And they that are Christ's have crucified the flesh with the affections and lusts. If we live in the Spirit, let us also walk in the Spirit."

A life that is changed is a life that is controlled by the Holy Spirit. The life that was once filled with evil, pride, and sin is changed to a life that is filled with the love of God and the love for one's neighbor.

Background

THE CHURCH IS COMING under increased pressure from many different groups as society's values continue to fall. Special interest groups that practice and promote immoral activity are working close with government to write new laws that legalize immoral activity. Out of fear from new legal restrictions churches have been changing their belief statements. In some case, these new belief statements include language that is actually contrary to Bible teaching. Some church pastors have said that the authors of the Bible did not understand the complex relationships today between men and women. In others words the Bible is not the inerrant word of God and God does not understand his creation, mankind.

It is generally agreed that the life we live on this earth is relativity short and is subject to many seen and unforeseen risks. Consequently, as Christians we need to discover and build on the strengths and talents God has blessed us with as soon as possible. Under God's guidance we need to establish goals and priorities that are in agreement with his plan for our life. God has a plan for each individual that will build on each individual's strengths and continue to bless each believer in many different ways. God is a very loving God who has washed away all sins for the believer and will open new opportunities to serve.

We need to use the time we have on this earth as wisely as possible to prepare ourselves for eternity with our Lord and Creator. We will all stand before our Lord and will need to be prepared to give an accounting of how we spent this time. God is both a loving God and a just God. As a loving God, God forced the Pharaoh of Egypt to release the Israelites from 400 years of slavery. As a just God, God required the Israelites to wander in the wilderness for 40 years after they refused to enter the Promised Land.

Today, Satan is attacking the church and Christians on many different fronts with the sole purpose of destroying all of mankind and all of God's creation. Satan is actually attacking our children and the schools they attend. Special interest groups are asking schools not to identify students as boys and girls. In fact, some interests groups are asking that the word family no longer be used.

The earth, the heavens and man were created by God for His purpose and for His glory. Every child is a blessing from God and is a source for life for all of mankind. Children are able to bring great joy to a family and a source for growth in loving kindness, patience, understanding, and forgiveness. 3 John 1:4 reads, "I have no greater joy than to hear that my children walk in truth." A parent's knowledge that their child will meet with them in heaven is overwhelming.

There are many important responsibilities related to raising a child. The teaching of Biblical truths begins at home within the family at an early age. Those simple truths will remain with the child for their lifetime. The family attending a church and Sunday school and the lessons learned will not be forgotten. The parent due to their age and experience will be able to provide protection and steer the child away from danger. Proverbs 22:6 reads, "Train up a child in the way he should go: and when he is old, he will not depart from it."

The most vulnerable segment of our population and the most fragile are the children. Unfortunately, man grossly underestimates the power and cleverness of Satan. Satan has been able to take control of Priests and church teachers to corrupt thousands of children. Satan is the great liar capable of spreading evil over the entire world.

The Catholic Church has paid an estimated $1 billion for thousands claiming they have been abused by Priests and teachers. The Boy Scouts of America have reached an estimated settlement of $850 million for over 84,000 cases for abuse. Deviant behavior has become so pervasive that it has affected the Woman's U.S. Olympic team. Deviant behavior is a disease that knows no bounds and infects all ages, sexes, and nationalities.

The Christian church has experienced many different challenges over the decades and is still in discussion over some theology. For example, Martin Luther who had great success in making the Bible available to the common man had issues with the Gospel of James.

James 2:26 reads, "For as the body without the spirit is dead, so faith without works is dead also."

The Apostle James is not suggesting salvation is earned by works completed by man. He was simply stating that a healthy tree will bear good fruit.

Matthew 7:16–17 reads, "Ye shall know them by their fruits. Do men gather grapes of thorns, or figs of thistles? Even so every good tree bringeth forth good fruit; but a corrupt tree bringeth forth evil fruit."

Jesus used the metaphor of a healthy tree and good fruit to explain that a man with faith in Jesus Christ will be responsible for good deeds.

My Father

My God is my loving Father. I love him with all my spiritual being, spirit, and soul. The soul and the spirit represent a major spiritual portion of the human being. Maintaining and ensuring a healthy soul and spirit requires a great deal of time and careful attention. 1 Thessalonians 5:19 reads, "Quench not the Spirit". The first step is to acknowledge the existence of God's Holy Spirit is well, present and actively involved in man's daily life. The result of God's Holy Spirit communing with another man's spirit may not be what we expect. We need to remember that God is in the business of making the impossible possible. We need to be careful and not to be quick to disregard new ideas or new opportunities without careful consideration.

As Christians we all have a long and difficult road to sanctification. However, there are many who are struggling with how to become a Christian. There are many different reasons why they struggle with the decision to ask Jesus to enter their life. Many look at those who profess to be Christians and see many sinful traits and see no reason to make a decision.

Luke 1:46–47 reads, "And Mary said, "My soul doth magnify the Lord, And my spirit hath rejoiced in God my Savior."

Every man and woman has a soul and the spirit that is able to communicate with God. There are those who refuse to believe in the existence of God and refuse to consider the existence of eternal life in heaven with their Creator.

The Christian has the knowledge and peace of knowing God has given them a life that has purpose and is part of God's divine plan.

Man and Woman

God created man from the dust of the earth. He created woman by placing man in a deep sleep and taking a rib from man to create woman.

Genesis 2:7 reads, "And the Lord God formed man of the dust of the ground, and breathed into his nostrils the breath of life; and man became a living soul."

All men were created by God with a physical body and living soul. Adam was placed in the garden to manage the garden. He was free to eat from every tree except for one tree.

Genesis 2:16–18 reads, "And the lord God commanded the man, saying, Of every tree of the garden thou mayest freely eat: But of the tree of the knowledge of good and evil, thou shalt not eat of it: for in the day that thou eatest thereof thou shalt surely die. And the Lord God said, it is not good that the man should be alone; I will make him a help meet for him."

God determined it was not good for man to be alone so he created woman by taking a rib from man. Women would always be a critical part of mankind and take on many life giving responsibilities. A perfect partnership was formed by God that would allow both man and woman to accomplish great things.

Genesis 2:21–22 reads, "And the Lord God caused a deep sleep to fall upon Adam, and he slept: and he took one of his ribs, and closed up the flesh instead thereof; And the rib, which the Lord God had taken from man, made he a woman, and brought her unto the man."

The creation of woman allowed man to leave his mother and father and to start a family with his chosen wife.

Genesis 2:24 reads, "Therefore shall a man leave his father and his mother, and shall cleave unto his wife; and they shall be one flesh."

God blessed Adam and Eve with a life that was filled with great beauty, a garden filled with delicious food, animals that filled their day with wonder, all with God's protective hand.

God also gave them freedom of choice that allowed them the freedom to make their own decisions. God placed only one restriction on them and that was not to eat from the tree of knowledge.

It seems ridiculous that Adam and Eve would risk losing all of their many blessings for the possibility of gaining godlike powers. Satan is aware of man's weaknesses of pride and greed and will tempt him at every opportunity.

We need to pray each day asking God for the strength to withstand Satan's many temptations.

1 Corinthian 10:13 reads, "There hath no temptation taken you but such as is common to man: but God is faithful, who will not suffer you to be tempted above that ye are able; but will with the temptation also make a way to escape, that ye may be able to bear it."

God is faithful and will provide the wisdom and strength for each of life's challenges.

God Is Both Loving and Just

Many people identify God as a loving God who does not disciple his followers. Nothing could be further from the truth. The Bible is filled with countless examples of God disciplining his people for not following his commandments. The Bible lists and identifies many sins. Sins will harm people in both a spiritual and physical way. The basic sins are worshiping other Gods, taking God name in vain, not remembering the Lord's day, not honoring your Father and Mother, to kill, adultery, to steal, false witnesses against your neighbor, covet your neighbor's wife, and covet your neighbor's possessions.

There are many more verses in the Bible that list sins.

Acts 15:20 reads, "But that we write unto them, that they abstain from pollutions of idols, and from fornication, and from things strangled, and from blood."

In this verse fornication is the sin that is associated with all sexual experiences encountered outside of marriage.

We worship a loving and just God. God is always there waiting to give us his love. God is also a just God that will discipline us if we sin. The type and time of the discipline we do not know.

1 John 1:9 reads, "If we confess our sins, he is faithful and just to forgive us our sins, and to cleanse us from all unrighteousness."

God- worshiping men have long been persecuted by pagans and pagan governments since the birth of man. It wasn't until Emperor Constantine in 337 AD that the persecution of all Christians and all God worshiping men began to slow down. However, we now see the pendulum began to swing in the other direction and the church and its members are now again under attack by pagans and pagan practices.

Psalm 46:1—3 reads, "God is our refuge and strength, a very present help in trouble. Therefore will not we fear, though the earth be removed, and though the mountains be carried into the midst of the sea; Thought the waters thereof roar and be troubled, though the mountains shake with the swelling thereof. Selah" (Consider these words)

We may encounter great danger and be placed in situations where we have no control, but as faithful believers we are always in God's hands.

Man Is Part of God's Creation

CREATION OF THE EARTH and the entire universe was created by God under his direction and according to his timetable. It is believed that angels too numerous to count shouted with joy as they witnessed God's creation unfold before them.

Job 38:7 reads, "When the morning stars sang together, and all the sons of God shouted for joy?"

It was God's angelic beings (the morning stars and sons of God) and all of God's ministering spirits that shouted with joy as they experienced God's majesty, almighty power and loving grace in the unfolding of creation.

Psalm 148: 1–3 reads, "Praise ye the Lord: Praise ye the Lord from the heavens: praise him in the heights. Praise ye him, all his angels: praise ye him, all his hosts. Praise ye him, sun and moon: praise him, all ye stars of light."

God created man in His own image with the ability to experience great joy and great sorrow, and is capable of great evil and great good. It isn't until a man realizes he needs to place all of his trust in God for direction and prays for the salvation of his soul that the Holy Spirit enters his life. At this point man experiences great joy that fills his soul and spirit and allows for the communion with man's Creator, God. The vast crevasse that was created between heaven and a fallen world when man sinned may be crossed with a prayer made in complete humility asking for forgiveness and submitting to God's commandments.

God created the angels as spiritual beings with free will and the ability to appear as humans. Their purpose is to worship God, protect and guide God's believers, and to ensure God's will is completed. Angels are present in the believer's life on a spiritual level as they communicate with the soul, spirit, heart and mind. Angels will also battle with evil spirits as they try to direct men from entertaining evil thoughts, engaging in evil acts, and doing harm to their fellow man.

God's angels are focused on carrying out God's commandments.

Deuteronomy 33:2 reads, "And he said, The Lord came from Sinai, and rose up from up from Seir unto them; he shined forth from mount Paran, and he came with ten thousands of saints: from his right hand went a fiery law for them."

God created the heavens and the earth and all those things that are present. He also created all those things that are not seen. The fact that we do not see something does not mean it does not exist. For example, we do not see disease, gravity, air, sound, many dangerous gases, and the dangerous rays from the sun, etc. Realizing our limited ability to see many things it is not unreasonable to think that there are many more things we do not see on a daily basis. An angel could be standing in front of us without our seeing the angel or hearing its message. It is only with God grace that those who have humbled themselves before the Lord and have open their hearts that are able to hear the message.

God created angels for a number of different reasons and are present as spiritual beings in different forms and shapes. They fill different purposes and fall into different hierarchies. Generally, when angels do appear they will warn people not to be afraid. They realize most people will be terrified and panic when seeing an angel.

Angels

God has created millions of millions of angels for the purpose of praising God and protecting His creation, man. As soon as man accepts the fact that God has sent His only Son to die on the Cross for all of man's sin that he opens the door to all of God's blessings. Many of these blessings in many ways are delivered by angels to man. A man's daily life may involve many angels that are providing communication, protection, and direction.

Psalm 34:7 reads, "The angel of the Lord encampeth around about them that fear him, and delivereth them."

Psalm 91:11 reads, "For he shall give his angels charge over thee, to keep thee in all thy ways."

There is a spiritual war that surrounds us each day. For the Christian, God has sent His angels to protect us from Satan and all his evil ways. Satan and his evil demons attack man each day in many different ways and from many different sources. It is God's angels that block or eliminate many of these dangers. Some of God's angels are extremely powerful and have the ability to remove any insurmountable road block or challenge.

However, we live in a fallen world that is full of dangers and we need to be prepared. We all will encounter some disappointments, sorrow, and pain. God will use some of these difficulties to teach us, mold us, and make us into people that are kind, understanding, and compassionate.

It is hard to believe that millions of people have rejected Christianity.

The angel of God and two other Angels appeared to Abraham as humans. They appeared to Abraham for the purpose of delivering a message about Sarah giving birth and the destruction of Sodom and Gomorrah. Abraham tried to negotiate with God about the destruction of Sodom and Gomorrah by pointing out that there were a number of righteous people living in the cities. Unfortunately, there were no righteous people living in the cities other than Lot and his family. The two angels traveled to Lot's home where they were attacked by a group of men. In this situation God directed the two angels to blind the attackers and provide protection for the removal of Lot and his family.

Genesis 19:15 reads, "And when the morning arose, then the angels hastened Lot, saying, Arise take thy wife, and thy two daughters, which are here; lest thou be consumed in the iniquity of the city."

The spiritual battle that was present in Sodom and Gomorrah is still going on today. Satan is still revolting against the all powerful God. However, today we do not see the spiritual battle that is raging around us. Most people are overwhelmed by the realities of today's world and live in a state of confusion created by Satan's many lies.

Ephesians 6:12 reads, "For we wrestle not against flesh and blood, but against principalities, against powers, against the rulers of the darkness of this world, against spiritual wickedness in high places."

My Great-GrandFather

My great-grandfather was born in Verona, Boone, Kentucky in 1883. He married Martha Metcalf in 1904 and they had 5 sons and 4 daughters. He was a farmer and was able to support the family through a number of difficult years including the great depression. At that time, large families worked as teams trying to bring the crops to the market along with other families in the community. Part of the family team effort also included using the system of bartering (exchanging time worked for goods or services).

My great-grandfather worked long hours and gained a reputation as an honest, trustworthy, and God fearing man. It is believed that Jim was responsible for bringing a church to the Tyner, Kentucky area. It is also believed that Jim assisted his children both financially and built houses for his children.

He was able to build integrity by being just with his business dealings and showing kindness to those in need. He lived his life in the service to the Lord for the purpose to bringing glory to God.

Proverbs 21:3 reads, "To do justice and judgment is more acceptable to the Lord than sacrifice."

Our words and deeds should reflect a heart that has surrendered to God's leading and grace.

Colossians 3:12 reads, "Put on therefore, as the elect of God, holy and beloved, bowels of mercies, kindness, humbleness of mind, meekness, long-suffering;"

We should reflect on what God has done for us and the love and grace that was given to us through the gift of His Son.

God forgave us for all of our sins of the past, present, and future. We should look at others with an attitude of forgiveness and charity.

We live our lives in a world that is always changing and bringing new challenges to all. However, as Christians we live out this life with the comfort of God's peace. God gives us the strength to push through all the challenges and persevere.

God has blessed us all with gifts that should be used to help others. Many of these gifts that are used to help others are related to service and compassion. Jesus looked at man with compassion and in some cases would heal those individuals of their many illnesses and in some cases would push evil spirits out from their bodies.

My great-grandfather was a deeply religious man that trusted in God to help him raise a large family during very difficult times. His family was extremely important to him and their love for each other and the love from a close net community made miracles possible during great challenges.

The Heart

The heart is a general term that is used throughout the Bible to describe man's innermost condition. The heart is the consolidation of environment, genetics, morals, and ethics. A strong family unit, Bible study, a nurturing environment will provide a person with many important personality traits (i.e., positivity, kindness, empathy). The genes that are passed down through the family will have impact on talents and learning abilities. Standards for appropriate behavior or morals are also passed down from families and friendships. Ethics or codes of conduct are learned from different organizations, church relationships or workplace environment.

However, if the Holy Spirit is invited into a person's life through a confession of faith a dramatic change will take place within a person's heart. If a person does not change his life then the Holy Spirit does not enter the person's life. Jesus connected with and associated with many sinners as he preached the gospel. His message was that salvation was available to all of mankind regardless of all the sins that a person may have committed.

Luke 6:43–45 reads, "For a good tree bringeth not forth corrupt fruit: neither doth a corrupt tree bring forth good fruit. For every tree is known by his own fruit. For of thorns men do not gather figs, nor of a bramble bush gather they grapes. A good man out of the good treasures of his heart bringeth forth that which is good, and an evil man out of the evil treasure of his heart bringeth forth that which is evil: for of the abundance of the heart his mouth speaketh."

A man who uses vile language is a man controlled by vile thoughts and has a deceitful heart. A man who performs vile acts and sins against God is not a man controlled by the Holy Spirit.

The Holy Spirit can heal damaged relationships, provide a deeper understanding of difficult relationships, and move people to open their minds to more effective solutions. The Holy Spirit can open doors where people will be exposed to new ideas, change values, and change attitudes.

Since the time of Adam and Eve's sin man has lived in a fallen state.

Jeremiah 17:9 reads, "The heart is deceitful above all things, and desperately wicked: who can know it?"

Recently, we have seen an increase in violence throughout the world as people, countries, and dictators invade other counties for wealth and greed. Many of these countries place little value on life and are willing to kill as many people as necessary to achieve their goals. The murder of innocent men, women and children will be judged severely by God in His time and place.

Prayer

The lives that we live out daily are in many ways influenced and determined in many respects by the decisions we make throughout our lives. Many of these decisions that are made are subject to Satan's influences and can have a devastating impact throughout our entire lives. The importance of prayer cannot be minimized and must be petitioned to God each day. Those individuals that decide to become Christians will experience the indwelling of God's Holy Spirit and will be given access to His direction. A Christian realizes that God has a plan for their lives and that plan will include using the gifts and talents that were given to them by God. The Christian will also experience the peace of God which cannot be explained in human terms.

Philippians 4:7 reads, "And the peace of God, which passeth all understanding, shall keep your hearts and minds through Christ Jesus."

Sin can infest a man's heart and soul to the point of blocking a man from seeing, hearing and realizing God's purpose for his life. We are in the middle of an ongoing spiritual war between good and evil. Each day should begin in prayer asking for God's direction, insight, and strength to resolve life's many issues and challenges.

Ephesians 6:12 reads, "For we wrestle not against flesh and blood, but against principalities, against powers, against the rulers of the darkness of this world, against spiritual wickedness in high places."

Satan is the great liar, deceiver, who is looking at every opportunity to rob man of God's blessings. The major objective of Satan is for man to destroy himself. He uses man's weaknesses (i.e., pride, lust, greed) to create a situation where man is at war with each other over positions and status. Man in his fallen state is easily convinced by Satan to act according to his wishes. As stated before, Satan is trying to convince man to destroy himself by any means possible.

1 Thessalonians 5:16–19 reads, "Rejoice evermore. Pray without ceasing. In every thing give thanks: for this is the will of God in Christ Jesus concerning you. Quench not the Spirit."

Ephesians 6:18 reads, "Praying always with all prayer and supplication in the Spirit, and watching thereunto with all perseverance and supplication for all saints;"

Our prayers need to be direct, filled with commitment, in obedience to His word and surrounded by God's Holy Spirit. We need to devote ourselves to prayer without ceasing and to call on God's strength to carry us to victory over Satan and his demons.

Heaven

The curtain that separates us from heaven is impossible for us to see through, but at the same time it is only a moment away from where we are. Jesus and his angels are able to cross from the physical to the spiritual with ease. Throughout history God has used angels to deliver important messages to his people. In some cases, angels that were selected to deliver these messages took on the form of a human. In many cases, those angels that have appeared began a message by saying "fear not". Obviously, in some cases an angel's appearance can be terrifying to some and is in need of some type of introduction that would warn a person of a possible difficult and disturbing sight. This warning may allow a person some time to quiet their soul and spirit to be open to hearing a message of importance.

Abraham was able to see that the men that appeared in front of his tent were angels. If these men were to appear before us today would we be able to determine if they were angels? Does any man today have the same close relationship Abraham had with God? God is the same today, yesterday, and forever.

The dream of these angels continually moving to and from heaven illustrates how God was continually with Jacob and how God's angels were continually delivering messages, blessings, and carrying out His will and plan for all of mankind.

In this situation, angels appeared to Jacob in a dream and provided some type of explanation as to how angels move from heaven to earth and back. In some respects a dream is the perfect method for God himself or an angel to communicate a message since the person dreaming is normally relaxed and is open to new ideas and suggestions.

God is the same today, yesterday and forever. God has revealed himself in dreams to man throughout history.

1 Kings 3:5 reads, "In Gibeon the Lord appeared to Solomon in a dream by night: and God said, Ask what I shall give thee."

This dream was extremely important because Solomon's answer in the dream pleased God and sealed the faith of all those that would experience Solomon's judgments.

1Kings 3:12 reads, "Behold, I have done according to thy words: lo, I have given thee a wise and an understanding heart; so that there was none like thee before thee, neither after thee shall any arise like unto thee."

This dream was created by God for the purpose of getting Solomon's attention and getting him to think about what was important in his life. Solomon's answer pleased God and resulted in Solomon receiving a blessing beyond measure. No man has ever been as wise as Solomon.

Another example of God using dreams was when God spoke to Joseph.

Matthew 1:20 reads, "But while he thought on these things, behold, the angel of the Lord appeared unto him in a dream, saying, Joseph, thou son of David, fear not to take unto thee Mary thy wife: for that which is conceived in her is of the Holy Ghost."

Joseph was greatly perplexed and under extremely pressure to find a solution that would resolve many social and religious problems. A dream was the perfect method by placing Joseph in a deep sleep that allowed God to communicate to Joseph a complicated and hard to believe message. Joseph had to disregard all that he understood of conception and place all of his faith in God's plan.

Most of the dreams we have on a daily basis have no meaning and in some cases are simply a review of past experiences. However, God may use a dream as a way to communicate a message to us. It is possible for God to use a dream to warn us of an impending danger, provide guidance in making a decision, or bring to light a forgotten fact. God's messages are endless and include endless possibilities.

Trusting in God

God sent his angel to Moses and the Israelites to protect and guide them as they traveled through the wilderness after escaping from Egypt and the Pharaoh.

Exodus 23:20–22 reads, "Behold, I send an angel before thee, to keep thee in the way, and to bring thee into the place which I have prepared. Beware of him, and obey his voice, provoke him not; for he will not pardon your transgressions: for my name is in him. But if thou shalt indeed obey his voice, and do all that I speak; then I will be an enemy unto thine enemies, and an adversary unto thine adversaries."

God warns Moses not to provoke this angel in any way, but to simply obey him as he provides directions. This angel speaks directly to Moses with God's authority and expects Moses to act without question and follow his directions to the letter. In this case there is no room for discussion or for any type of compromise.

God knew Moses and his weaknesses. When God first spoke to Moses in Midian he lacked many character traits that would make him a great leader. Moses said he wasn't good enough to lead the Israelites, he wasn't an eloquent speaker, and he wasn't qualified. God met Moses where he was and gave Moses the knowledge and character traits needed to be successful. Moses learned that he needed to trust God for the strength and wisdom and to move forward and stop making excuses. If you depend on God for your strength and wisdom he will direct his angels to protect you in many ways.

Psalm 91:9–12 reads. "Because thou hast made the Lord, which is my refuge, even the most high, thy habitation; There shall no evil befall thee, neither shall any plague come nigh thy dwelling. For he shall give his angels charge over thee, to keep thee in all thy ways. They shall bear thee up in their hands, lest thou dash thy foot against a stone."

The Lord came to Moses with thousands of angels in preparing the law at Sinai.

Psalm 68:17 reads, "The chariots of God are twenty thousand, even thousands of angels: the Lord is among them, as in Sinai, in the holy place."

Deuteronomy 33:1–3 reads, "And this is the blessing, wherewith Moses the man of God blessed the children of Israel before his death. And he said, The Lord came from Sinai, and rose up from Seir unto them; he shined forth from mount Paran, and he came with ten thousands of saints: from his right hand went a fiery law for them. Yea, he loved the people; all his saints are in thy hand: and they sat down at thy feet; everyone shall receive of thy words."

Angels are God's messengers and often accompany Him during important events. The angels that accompany God are powerful and holy. They saw the fall of Satan, the fall of man, and God's judgment and punishment. They understand and love the scriptures and righteousness.

We pray each day thanking God for His many blessings and protection.

God's Creation

GOD CREATED MAN OUT of His love and grace and made it possible for all to spend eternity with Him. It is estimated that 100 billion people have lived on this world with over seven billion living today. However, it was God's sacrifice that made it possible for the sins for these billions of people to be forgiven with a decision to believe in God and the sacrifice of His Son. God sacrificed His only Son and raised Him after three days to overcome death and the power of Satan. The scope and wonder of this miracle is beyond our comprehension. Only one person was able to live his life on this world without sin and that was God's Son, Jesus Christ. Man's faith and love for the One True Almighty God and His Son opens the door for salvation for all of mankind. Today, we are still in the middle of a war between good and evil. God has deployed His many angels that are continually protecting us from Satan and his many demons. In most cases, we do not know of these attacks or understand how they are affecting our daily lives.

Ephesians 6:12 reads, "For we wrestle not against flesh and blood, but against principalities, against powers, against the rulers of the darkness of this world, against spiritual wickedness in high places."

Satan is the great liar, deceiver, who is looking at every opportunity to rob man of God's blessings. The major objective of Satan is for man to destroy himself. He uses man's weaknesses (i.e., pride, lust, greed) to create a situation where man is at war with each other over positions and status. Man in his fallen state is easily convinced by Satan to act according to his wishes. As stated before, Satan is trying to convince man to destroy himself by any means possible.

It is believed that the Angel of the Lord is a special angel that God uses in special situations to deliver important messages. The Angel of the Lord spoke directly to Moses to ensure the release of the Israelites from Egypt and the Pharaoh. The release of the Israelites from Egypt would require

God's power and wisdom to make the Pharaoh give up an extremely valuable asset to Egypt. The Israelites represented a major portion of Egypt's slave labor force and were responsible for building many the Pharaoh's massive structures.

The other angel that is mentioned is the destroyer (angel of death) that will visit those homes without the blood of a lamb posted on their doors.

Exodus 12: 23 reads, "For the Lord will pass through to smite the Egyptians; and when he seeth the blood upon the lintel, and on the two side posts, the Lord will pass over the door, and will not suffer the destroyer to come in unto your houses to smite you."

The Israelites were required to sacrifice a lamb without blemish and place the blood from the lamb on the top door support and on the two sides of the door to protect their first born from the angel of death.

God sent His angel to go ahead of the Israelites to provide protection and direction as they traveled through the wildness to the Promised Land of Canaan. We need to accept God's gift of protection and trust in the Holy Spirit.

Hebrew 1:14 reads, "Are they not all ministering spirits, sent forth to minister for them who shall be heirs of salvation?"

Angels work for God in providing protection for the believer. Angels assist the believer in many different ways in avoiding sin on their path to eternal life. The angel is able to communicate to God in all possible situations. The decision made by the believer to accept God's invitation for salvation allows angels to minister to the believer in many different ways. As believers we are protected by angels on a daily basis as we follow God's purpose and will for our life.

A New Covenant

THE ANGEL OF THE covenant was an angel of great power that could destroy many armies and could bring great fear to anyone that would dare to resist. God tells Moses and Aaron to obey this angel's commands and do not provoke him with any resistance. This angel has God's name within him and represents God's direction.

Jeremiah prophesied (640BC-586BC) that a new covenant would confirm the blessings of the old and the unchangeable laws of God. Under the new covenant God's law would be written on the hearts of man where God's love may be experienced within all man.

Jeremiah 31:31–34 reads, "Behold, the days come, saith the Lord, that I will make a new covenant with the house of Israel, and with the house of Judah. Not according to the covenant that I made with their fathers in the day that I took them by the hand to bring them out of the land of Egypt; which my covenant they brake, although I was a husband unto them, saith the lord: But this shall be the covenant that I will make with the house of Israel; After those days, saith the Lord, I will put my law in their inward parts, and write it in their hearts; and will be their God, and they shall be my people. And they shall teach no more every man his neighbor, and every man his brother, saying, Know the Lord: for they shall all know me, from the least of them unto the greatest of them, saith the Lord: for I will forgive their iniquity, and I will remember their sin no more."

The Israelites had failed during their bondage in Egypt and failed to keep God's law in the wilderness. Christ announced in the upper room that a new covenant would be sealed with His blood on the cross. The new covenant allowed the Holy Spirit to enter into a man's spirit and provide moral direction and a realization of Gods' mercy and grace.

Samuel's Special Relationship With God

SAMUEL'S LIFE BEGAN AS an answer to prayer. Hannah his mother had prayed for many years before giving birth to Samuel. At an early age, Samuel was placed under the religious training of Eli a leader and high priest.

1 Samuel 3:16—17 reads, "Then Eli called Samuel, and said, Samuel, my son. And he answered, Here am I. And he said, What is the thing that the Lord hath said unto thee? I pray thee hide it not from me: God do so to thee, and more also, if thou hide any thing from me of all the things that he said unto thee."

Eli realized Samuel had a special relationship with God and that God was providing Samuel with important information. Samuel grew in his relationship with God and faithfully provided God's messages to the people of Israel. Samuel loved God and obeyed Him without question. It was this type of commitment that created within him unquestionable integrity.

God used Samuel to communicate His messages in many ways. Samuel anointed both King Saul and King David thereby moving Israel's leadership from Judges to Kings.

1 Samuel 15:10–11 reads, "Then came the word of the Lord unto Samuel, saying, It repenteth me that I have set up Saul to be King: for he is turned back from following me, and hath not performed my commandments. And it grieved Samuel; and he cried unto the Lord all night."

Again, God speaks directly to Samuel and tells Samuel that He regrets setting up Saul as King because of his disobedience.

1 Samuel 16:1 reads, "And the Lord said unto Samuel, How long wilt thou mourn for Saul, seeing I have rejected him from reigning over Israel? Fill thine horn with oil, and go, I will send thee to Jesse the Beth-Iehemite: for I have provided me a king among his sons."

1 Samuel 16:10–13 reads, "Again, Jesse made seven of his sons to pass before Samuel. And Samuel said unto Jesse, The Lord hath not chosen these.

And Samuel said unto Jesse, Are here all thy children? And he said, There remaineth yet the youngest, and, behold, he keepeth the sheep. And Samuel said unto Jesse, Send and fetch him: for we will not sit down till he come hither. And he sent, and brought him in. Now he was ruddy, and withal of a beautiful countenance, and goodly to look to. And the Lord said, Arise, anoint him: for this is he. Then Samuel took the horn of oil, and anointed him in the midst of his brethren: and the Spirit of the Lord came upon David from that day forward. So Samuel rose up, and went to Ramah."

God had selected David not because of his experience, wealth, knowledge, position, or his physical stature. God selected David because of his heart and his willingness to obey God's direction. David loved God with all his heart, soul and mind. He was eager to obey God's commands and lived to please God.

God's Direction

DAVID WAS A GREAT King because of his great relationship with God. It is generally believed that David was anointed by Samuel to be king very early in his life. Some believe David was only ten to thirteen years of age when anointed to be king by Samuel. However, becoming king would not occur until David reached the age of thirty and endured a great deal of challenges and hardships over many years. Initially, David was accepted by King Saul as a musician and a soldier and was not considered a threat to his reign.

However, Saul eventually learned of David's secret anointment by Samuel and plotted to have David eliminated. Consequently, David spent many years running and hiding in the wilderness in an effort to escape capture by Saul's soldiers.

God was faithful and protected David throughout these many years in the wilderness. During these years, David learned that the first response to any issues was to worship God and ask for His blessings and direction.

1 Kings 14:8 reads, ". . . and yet thou hast not been as my servant David, who kept my commandments, and who followed me with all his heart, to do that only which was right in mine eyes;"

David became a great king, but not without many grueling years of distress and despair. It was only through these many difficult years that David learned how much God loved him and cared for him.

God's love for David came in the form of forgiveness, grace and mercy. David, in turn showed this same love, mercy and forgiveness as King of Israel. David had learned to place his complete trust in God and no longer reacted to attacks about his honor and position. David understood that God was in charge of his life and God would protect him from those who would try to discredit him in any way. In fact, God's response to any injustice or unprovoked action against David was much more severe than anything David could have contrived.

David was also a great warrior that expanded the kingdom and was able to build a huge army that was respected throughout the region. David was able to capture Jerusalem back from the Jebusites and made it into the capital of Israel.

2 Samuel 8:11–15 reads, "Which also king David did dedicate unto the Lord, with the silver and gold that he had dedicated of all the nations which he subdued; Of Syria, and of Moab, and of the children of Ammon, and of th Philistines, and of Amalek, and of the spoil of Hadadezer, son of Rehob, king of Zobah. And David gat him a name when he returned from smiting of the Syrians in the valley of salt, being eighteen thousand men. And he put garrisons in Edom; throughout all Edom put he garrisons, and all they of Edom became David's servants. And the Lord preserved David whithersoever he went. And David reigned over all Israel; and David executed judgment and justice unto all his people."

David with his army was able to bring unification back to the twelve tribes. Israel and Judah once again became one country, Israel. Jerusalem became the location for the Temple of God and the Ark.

Acts 13:22 reads, "And when he had removed him, he raised up unto them David to be their king; to whom also he gave testimony, and said, I have found David the son of Jesse, a man after mine own heart, which shall fulfill all my will."

It was David whom God selected to bring unification back to Israel. Even though David was a sinner, God was able to use him in some powerful ways. David was a man who was humble, God fearing, repentant, and who spent much of his life trying to please God in song, words, and action.

David's Heart

David's humble prayer is one that acknowledges God's greatness and gives thanks for God's many blessings.

2 Samuel 7:18–21 reads, "Then went King David in, and sat before the Lord, and he said, Who am I, O Lord God? And what is my house, that thou hast brought me hitherto? And this was yet a small thing in thy sight, O Lord God; but thou hast spoken also of thy servant's house for a great while to come. And is this the manner of man, O Lord God? And what can David say more unto thee? for thou. Lord God, knowest thy servant. For thy word's sake, and according to thine own heart, hast thou done all these great things, to make thy servant know them.

David begins his prayer in complete submission and makes it clear that he is not worthy of God's blessings. David's heart is open, waiting to be obedient to God's word.

David was a unique, obedient, highly talented individual that God was able to mold into a great king. David's training was difficult and lasted for many years before God allowed him to be king. This training changed David's perspective as to how he viewed and evaluated different people in different situations. He became more sensitive to others, more compassionate, and gained greater control over his character.

God's love for David and the great accomplishments and the great success of his kingdom paved the way for the bloodline for the Messiah. God's love for mankind is overwhelming and is difficult to comprehend. David's sins were numerous and serious and cannot be minimized in any way. However, like David, we can ask God for the forgiveness for all of our sins and become obedient to His commands.

David was a man who deeply regretted his sin and fell on his face asking God for forgiveness and mercy. David feared he may lose his relationship with God's Holy Spirit and pleaded and begged for days for forgiveness.

God worked with King David as He works with us today. God loved King David because he was a man after God's own heart. Even though David was guilty of many sins he always remained a faithful worshiper of God. David had a passion for God and he asked for forgiveness for all of his sins with great sincerity and humility.

God loves the sinner, but hates the sin. Jesus told the adulterous women at the well to "go and sin no more." Man was given free will and has the power to sin or not to sin.

James 1:13–15 reads, "Let no man say when he is tempted, I am tempted of God: for God cannot be tempted with evil, neither tempteth he any man: But every man is tempted, when he is drawn away of his own lust, and enticed. Then when lust hath conceived, it bringeth forth sin: and sin, when it is finished, bringeth forth death."

We all live as fallen man and have sins that live inside us. It is our decision to either accept these sinful thoughts and act on them or reject them and take control of our thoughts and actions.

John 14:15 reads, "If ye love me, keep my commandments."

If you love God you will live a life that is based on following God's commandments and showing His love to others.

God's Love

G OD ALLOWED MANY NATIONS to invade and destroy the land of Israel because of their failure to remain a righteous people that worshipped the one true God.

God is the same yesterday, today, and forever. God loved the land of Israel and the people of Israel and disciplined them for their failures. God loves His children and will discipline those whom He loves. God will allow the pain from a fallen world to discipline those whom have failed to live a righteous life.

There is a direct relationship between sin and discipline. There is also a price to be paid for those sins.

Man is in a fallen state and lives in a fallen world. The only person that lived a sinless life in this world was Jesus Christ. The wages of sin is death and Jesus paid that debt in full on the cross. Jesus bore the wrath of God for all of man's sin so that man would not suffer the price for man's sin. Therefore, 1 John 1:9 reads, "If we confess our sins, he faithful and just to forgive us our sins, and to cleanse us from all unrighteousness."

However, God loves His creation, mankind, and continually works to form mankind into His likeness. The challenges of life will chasten mankind and is designed to bring man into a closer relationship with God. Any unclean thought, word, or action will be met with God's discipline.

Christians live in the hope of things to come. What we see is temporary, but what is unseen, the Spiritual, lives forever.

Ezekiel was a prophet and priest from Israel who wrote about the destruction of Jerusalem and the exile of the Israelites to Babylon. At a young age Ezekiel prophesied the judgment of Israel because it trusted in foreign gods and other pagan practices. Ezekiel's prophecies also included hope and the eventual return to Jerusalem and Judah.

Ezekiel 1:1 reads, "Now it came to pass in the thirtieth year, in the fourth month, in the fifth day of the month, as I was among the captives by the river of Chebar, that the heavens were open, and I saw visions of God."

Ezekiel 1:3 reads, "The word of the Lord came expressly unto Ezekiel the priest, the son of Buzi, in the land of the Caldeans by the river Chebar; and the hand of the Lord was there upon him."

Ezekiel's message stressed the importance of worshiping the one true God and that the worship of idols by the people resulted in the exile to Babylon. Ezekiel's prophecy began when he was exiled to Babylon and continued for approximately twenty years.

God spoke through Ezekiel to deliver the message that the worship of idols and other sins was the cause for their exile to Babylon. Ezekiel's prophecy and message was met with rejection and displeasure because he reminded them of their sin.

Ezekiel 2:6 reads, "And thou, son of man, be not afraid of them, neither be afraid of their words, though briers and thorns be with thee, and thou dost dwell among scorpions: be not afraid of their words, not be dismayed at their looks, though they be a rebellious house."

God encouraged Ezekiel not to be afraid and to continue to deliver God's message to those that were exiled. The task was difficult and dangerous and God would provide him with the words to be used. God also provided Ezekiel with additional strength, confidence, and determination.

Noah's Faith

It is impossible to please God without faith. The Christian and his life are based on the faith that God does exist and that he is all-powerful, all-knowing, and is everywhere.

Hebrews 11:6 reads, "But without faith it is impossible to please him: for he that cometh to God must believe that he is, and that he is a rewarder of them that diligently seek him."

Hebrews 11:7 reads, "By faith Noah, being warned of God of things not seen as yet, moved with fear, prepared an ark to the saving of his house; by the which he condemned the world, and because heir of the righteousness which is by faith."

Noah walked with God and obeyed God's commands. Noah obeyed God out of faith and fear knowing that God is an all-powerful God capable of flooding the entire earth if He wishes. God actually told Noah how to build the ark and what type of tree to be used for its construction.

The Apostle Peter spoke of how God is a just God and how He will judge those who sin.

2 Peter 2:4–7 reads, "For if God spared not the angels that sinned, but cast them down to hell, and delivered them into chains of darkness, to be reserved unto judgment; And spared not the old world, but saved Noah the eighth person, a preacher of righteousness, bringing in the flood upon the world of the ungodly; And turning the cities of Sodom and Gomorrah into ashes condemned them with an overthrow, making them an example unto those that after should live ungodly; And delivered just Lot, vexed with the filthy conversation of the wicked:"

Noah lived a life of a righteous man in the old world that was completely consumed by evil. It is believed that he and his family lived a life under extreme pressure from people that mocked and ridiculed them for many years as they built the ark.

Living a righteous life in an ungodly world is difficult. However, God made a way of escape for the Christian that believes in the gift of God's Only Son, Jesus Christ.

We will all stand in front of our Creator and be judged for our sins. However, the Christian because of his faith in Jesus Christ will have his sins forgiven.

Why Me

Those that were exiled to Babylon with Ezekiel were confused and looking for answers and the reasons for their exile. People today are asking the same question that was being asked by God's people in Ezekiel's time. Why me or why is this happening now? God loves His creation and is continually directing them and encouraging them to live a righteous life. God uses the pressures and hardships of this life to bring us to the realization that sin is real and needs to be confessed. We are a work-in-process and God is molding us into his likeness. This process is difficult and requires a real sense of self and the willingness to stop and evaluate your life

Psalm 137:1–3 reads, "By the rivers of Babylon, there we sat down, yea, we wept, when we remembered Zion. We hanged our harps upon the willows in the midst thereof. For there they that carried us away captive required of us a song; and they that wasted us required of us mirth, saying, Sing us one of the songs of Zion."

As Ezekiel, we may be surrounded by scorpions waiting to sting us with their venomous words or actions. However, we serve an all powerful God who controls both good and evil in this world and has a specific plan for each of us.

2 Corinthians 4:17–18 reads, "For our light affliction, which is but for a moment, worketh for us a far more exceeding and eternal weight of glory; While we look not at the things which are seen: but at the things which are not seen: for the things which are seen are temporal; but the things which are not seen are eternal."

God's love for us has no limits and restrictions. God is focused on our spiritual life and in molding us into a Christ-like person. His goal is to make us into individuals that produce fruit. The master of the vineyard bruins the vines to ensure the plant is healthy and continues to produce fruit. God is at work in our lives using discipline to cut away bad attitudes, unhealthy life practices, and many other sinful distractions that would prevent the production of healthy fruit. God is looking to mold into us Christ-like characteristics and righteousness.

God is a gardener who prunes away the dead branches that do not produce fruit. The pruning strengthens the plant and allows new branches to grow and produce more fruit. The fruit of the spirit is love, joy, and peace. Christians are identified by the love they show to others.

God's Messengers

It is believed that the archangel Gabriel was sent to help Daniel interpret dreams.

Daniel 8:15–18 reads, "And it came to pass, when I, even I Daniel, had seen the vision, and sought for the meaning, then, behold, there stood before me as the appearance of a man. And I heard a man's voice between the banks of Ulai, which called, and said, Gabriel, make this man to understand the vision. So he came near where I stood: and when he came, I was afraid, and fell upon my face: but he said unto me, Understand, O son of man, for at the time of the end shall be the vision. Now as he was speaking with me, I was in a deep sleep on my face toward the ground: but he touched me, and set me upright."

God in this situation sends the archangel Gabriel to communicate to Daniel. It is believed that Gabriel places Daniel in a deep sleep and allowed Daniel access to the spiritual realm.

God also sent His angels to protect Daniel from the lions that were locked in the den with him.

Daniel 6:22 reads, "My God hath sent his angel, and hath shut the lion's mouths, that they have not hurt me: forasmuch as before him innocency was found in me; and also before thee, O King, have I done no hurt."

The angels of God are powerful and capable of controlling wild animals and man. Angels of God are capable of controlling man in many different ways without their knowledge.

God also sent his angels to protect Shadrach, Meshach, and Abednego in the fiery furnace.

Daniel 3:28 reads, "Then Nebuchadnezzar spake, and said, Blessed be the God of Shadrach, Meshach, and Abednego, who hath sent his angel, and delivered his servants that trusted in him, and have changed the king's word, and yielded their bodies, that they might not serve nor worship any god, except their own God."

These three men refused to worship the golden image Nebuchadnezzar had made. God's angel prevented the fire from harming these three men for a number of reasons. God sent his angel to protect these men to show to Nebuchadnezzar that the one true Almighty God is able to protect men from many dangers, God recognizes men of strong faith, and God is loving and faithful to his believers.

God will send His angels into difficult situations to protect His believers. When all possible solutions within human reason have been exhausted, God will send His angels to resolve the problem. The issues and problems are never the same and solutions are unique.

It was Daniel's humble and continual prayers that made God respond to Daniel's requests for understanding. God hears our fervent prayers and may respond by sending an angel to communicate information by allowing access to the spiritual realm. Daniel was a faithful servant that spent much of his prayer life on his knees pleading for forgiveness and wisdom.

Jeremiah 29:13 reads, "And ye shall seek me, and find me, when ye shall search for me with all your heart."

Daniel's prayers were heard and God sent his angels to minister so that he may get a better understanding of the spiritual realm.

We need to keep an open mind and allow the Holy Spirit to direct our path whenever possible.

Spiritual World

Elisha prayed that the Lord would open the eyes of a young servant.

2 Kings 6:17 reads, "And Elisha prayed, and said, Lord, I pray thee, open his eyes, that he may see, And the Lord opened the eyes of the young man; and he saw: and, behold, that mountain was full of horses and chariots of fire round about Elisha."

God allowed this young servant of Elisha to see the spiritual realm. It was a world that was amazing that was filled with angels and with many other things impossible to describe.

The spirit of God teaches us many things that are freely given and are not of this world. The nature man can only see the things of this world as they relate to science and considers all spiritual things as foolish.

1 Corinthians 2:9–10 reads, "But as it is written, Eye hath not seen, not ear heard, neither have entered into the heart of man, the things which God hath prepared for them that loved him. But God hath revealed them unto us by His Spirit: for the Spirit searcheth all things, yes, the deep things of God."

Society and the culture of that day had fallen to great depths. It was common for people to worship idols in the hope of receiving a good crop and healthy animals. Their superstitions made them easy prey for corrupt rulers like King Ahab and Jezebel who promoted this worship of pagan gods by building monuments and temples for Baal and others. In addition, hundreds of priests and oracles were employed to convince people to sacrifice animals, money, and children to these false gods for rain, sun, and prosperity.

God's Divine Glory

THE NAME ELIJAH MEANS "My God is Yahweh." It is estimated he was born in 900 BC at Tishba in the Gilead region (located in the northern kingdom of Israel) during the time of King Ahab and King Ahaziah. It was said, he was born with an angel at his side that provided a fabric of fire that surrounded him. We are told his appearance was rough due to the fact he lived off the land and would rest in caves. However, he had a relationship with God that few men have ever experienced. As a Jewish priest, Elijah lived a life in complete obedience to God's will that resulted in him seeing and prophesying events that were impossible to be foreseen by any other human being. He grew to be one of the most important prophets in the world and experienced first-hand blessings directly from God.

God used Elijah as a prophet to reveal and communicate His purpose in reflecting His divine glory.

Deuteronomy 18:18–19 reads, "I will raise them up a Prophet from among their brethren, like unto thee, and will put my words in his mouth; and he shall speak unto them all that I shall command him. And it shall come to pass, that whosoever will not hearken unto my words which he shall speak in my name, I will require it of him."

God raised up many prophets among the people for the purpose of providing an intercessor between God and man. Like Moses, God spoke directly to Elijah and directed him as to what to say to King Ahab.

As Moses, Elijah travels through the wilderness with God's direction and His angels. For 40 days and 40 nights he traveled to Mount Horeb in the Sinai. It is believed this is the same place where God made his covenant with Israel and gave Moses the 10 commandments.

1 Kings 19:9–10 reads, "And he came thither unto a cave, and lodged there; behold, the word of the Lord came to him, and he said unto him, What doest thou here, Elijah? And he said, I have been very jealous for the

Lord God of hosts: for the children of Israel have forsaken thy covenant, thrown down thine altars, and slain thy prophets with the sword; and I, even I only, am left; and they seek my life, to take it away."

God asked Elijah what he was doing in this cave as if to say there is much to be done and this was not the way to get His work accomplished. God was very patient and loving with His servant and knew what he had experienced. The Lord is merciful, gracious, longsuffering, and is full of goodness and truth.

1Kings 19:15–16 reads, "And the Lord said unto him, Go, return on thy way to the wilderness of Damascus: and when thou comest, anoint Hazael to be King over Syria. And Jehu the son of Nimshi shalt thou anoint to be king over Israel: and Elisha the son of Shaphat of Abel-meholah shalt thou anoint to be prophet in thy room."

God was instructing Elijah by saying He will determine how, when, and where Ahab will be confronted by his sins. God is in control and he will determine when evil is released and the penalty for sin is paid. In this case, because Ahab had repented and publically displayed his remorse God did provide a temporary stay. However, Ahab was later killed and his sins were transferred to his sons who were also killed. Confession of our sins and praying for our forgiveness is important aspect of being a Christian.

Christians today are under God's grace due to His overwhelming love, love we are not worthy of, and a love we cannot comprehend. God allowed His only Son to die on a cross to give all of mankind the opportunity to spend eternity with Him in heaven. Today we are dependent on the Holy Spirit to help us to recognize our sins and make changes that will place us in communion with our Creator.

Enemies

THROUGHOUT HISTORY, ISRAEL AND the Jewish people had a number of enemies that would invade Israel and steal her treasures and land. Ben-Hadad the king of Syria (885BC—860BC) had a great army and the support of thirty two other kings in the area. King Ben-Hadad was jealous of Israel's riches and wanted Samaria and its rich land and sent a messenger to King Ahab demanding that King Ahab turn over all his gold and property. King Ben-Hadad and the people of Syria worshiped a number of pagan gods and were greatly dependent on hundreds of false prophets for direction in many areas of their lives. However, God sent an unnamed prophet of God to King Ahab of Israel to explain that God would not allow his army to be defeated by the Syrians. The fact that this prophet told Ahab what was going to happen, makes it impossible for Ahab not to acknowledge it was God who was in control of the outcome of this war. God saved King Ahab from a certain defeat and death. God wanted Ahab and all men to acknowledge that God was in control and to place their trust in Him and not on themselves.

Ahab was also involved in a conflict over a vineyard owned by Naboth. The vineyard was located in Jezreel next to Ahab's palace in Samaria. Ahab wanted to purchase the vineyard, but Naboth refused because it was promised as part of a family inheritance. Ahab was displeased and complained to Jezebel. Jezebel (Satan incarnate) developed a scheme that would place Naboth in a very difficult position. Jezebel paid for witnesses that claimed that Naboth had blasphemed God and the King. The people when they heard of this blasphemy claim took Naboth out of the city and stoned him to death. Due to custom Naboth sons were also killed thereby allowing the King to lay claim to the vineyard.

As with Moses, God required Elijah to confront the ruler of the land, in this case Ahab King of Israel. Elijah found Ahab in the vineyard of Naboth who was killed due to Jezebel's scheming and lying.

After the death of King Ahab, Ahaziah his son assumed control of northern Israel and Jehoshaphat maintains control over Judah. The death of a King would normally leave some vacuum in control and rebellion would normally break out. Mesha king of Moab (area east of the Dead Sea and now western Jordan) was successful in a rebellion over high taxes. Ahaziah became sick and requested an oracle of Baal that was a rebellion to the worship of the God of Israel. It was this rebellion by King Ahaziah and the following of his mother (Jezebel) in the worship of Baal that provoked the anger of the Lord God of Israel.

2 Kings 1:3–4 reads, "But the angel of the Lord said to Elijah the Tishbite, Arise, go up to meet the messengers of the King of Samaria, and say unto them, Is it not because there is not a God in Israel, that ye go to inquire of Baal-zebub the god of Ekron? Now therefore thus saith the Lord, Thou shalt not come down from that bed on which thou art gone up, but shalt surely die. And Elijah departed."

The angel of the Lord speaks directly to Elijah as he did with Moses and commands him to confront King Ahaziah. The angel of the Lord speaks as God, executes the power of God, and identifies himself as God. Those that see him fear for their lives because they recognize the power and presence of God himself. King Ahaziah had deliberately turned from the Lord God of Israel and worshiped Baal for the healing of his aliment. His worship of Baal was responsible for hardening the hearts of the people against the God of Israel.

God is the same today, yesterday and forever. How God deals with our enemies and sin is only known by Him. In some cases God's punishment of our enemies is much more severe then what we could imagine. However, our focus should not be of the present but on the future.

John: 14:1–2 reads, "Let not your heart be troubled: ye believe in God, believe also in me. In my Father's house are many mansions: if it were not so, I would have told you. I go to prepare a place for you."

God Is in Control

God revealed to Elijah that he will soon depart from this earth and needs to prepare Elisha to take his place. Elisha's main task would be to carry on Elijah's mission to stop the worship of idols. Elisha then asked Elijah to provide him with a double portion of his spiritual power and understanding. Obviously, this is only possible through God's will.

Elijah's reputation was great among the prophets and he shared his vision with the guild of prophets and priests of Israel. This guild of 50 prophets began to follow Elijah at a distance to both provide protection and to bear witness to the prophecy of his departure.

We are limited in our ability to understand all of God's plans and actions that take place within a man's life here on earth and in heaven. This was especially true of Elijah who like Moses spoke directly with God. Elijah was an extraordinary man that had an extraordinary relationship with God Almighty. He was chosen of God to be His representative and experienced God's protection and care.

2 Kings 2:11 reads, "And it came to pass, as they still went on, and talked, that, behold, there appeared a chariot of fire, and horses of fire, and parted them both asunder; and Elijah went up by a whirlwind into heaven."

God is in control and He will decide what will transpire on earth and within each man's life. In this case, God decided that it was time for Elijah to depart this earth and go to heaven, so He took him. At this time, God determined the mission of confronting the pagan idol worshipers would be passed on to Elisha. So the mission and the mantle were then passed on to Elisha.

Elijah was a man with many human frailties, but his heart and soul was devoted completely to the worship and praise of the Lord God Almighty of Israel. The governments, its rulers, were all corrupt and wanted to continue to enslave it's people to worship Baal and other idols for the purpose of extorting money and other valuables for the promise of good fortune.

God knew the heart of Elijah and accepted him as His messenger to deliver God's voice to a people that were lost in the worship of pagan idols.

God loved Elijah regardless of his many human frailties. He was at times completely dependent on God for food, shelter, and protection. His single purpose in life was to please God with His prophecies. He was God's messenger and he was God's humble obedient servant. He was truly a unique individual that lived off the land and took shelter wherever God provided it.

We live in a world that is highly judgmental and has little time for those who do not agree with the world's morals and standards. God sees each person as an individual and He provides blessings that are best for that individual.

God stands at the door and is waiting for each individual to ask for acceptance. Heaven belongs to those who have trusted God for their salvation.

Matthew 7:7 reads, "Ask, and it shall be given you; seek, and ye shall find; knock, and it shall be opened unto you:"

John 13:1 reads, "Now before the feast of the Passover, when Jesus knew that his hour was come that he should depart out of this world unto the Father, having loved his own which were in the world, he loved them unto the end."

Jesus' life, teachings and his death were a gift to all of mankind. God was in complete control of all the events that lead to Jesus' death. There is no greater love then the love God gave to his followers with the gift of His Son.

God's Plan

It is believed that Jeremiah was born and grew up in a family that was involved in the Temple at Jerusalem. He was approached by God to become a prophet at an early age. He was outspoken as a child and highly critical of the priests and those involved in the Temple. He was born in the city of Anathoth which was located just north of Jerusalem. His prophetic ministry lasted about 40 years.

Jeremiah 1:5–9 reads, "Before I formed thee in the belly I knew thee; and before thou comest forth out of the womb I sanctified thee, and I ordained thee a prophet unto the nations. Then said I, Ah, Lord God! Behold, I cannot speak: for I am a child. But the Lord said unto me, Say not, I am a child: for thou shalt go to all that I shall send thee, and whatsoever I command thee thou shalt speak. Be not afraid of their faces: for I am with thee to deliver thee, saith the Lord. Then the Lord put forth his hand, and touched my mouth. And the Lord said unto me, Behold, I have out my words in thy mouth."

God's plan for Jeremiah's life as a prophet was determined before Jeremiah's birth. God spoke directly to Jeremiah and explained to him that He (God) would be with him and protect him from his enemies. As Moses and many others, Jeremiah was fearful and did not believe he was capable of handling that much responsibility. Jeremiah was commanded by God to deliver a message that was highly critical of the priests and the people living at that time. The sins of the people would eventually lead to the destruction of Judah.

Jeremiah 32:15 reads, "For thus saith the Lord of hosts, the God of Israel; Houses and fields and vineyards shall be possessed again in this land."

Lamentations 3:21–26 reads, "This I recall to my mind, therefore have I hope. It is of the Lord's mercies that we are not consumed because his compassions fail not. They are new every morning: great is thy faithfulness.

The Lord is my portion, saith my soul; therefore will I hope in him. The Lord is good unto them that wait for him, to the soul that seeketh him. It is good that a man should both hope and quietly wait for the salvation of the Lord."

Jeremiah was a strong and courageous prophet who trusted in God for his wisdom and direction. Even under great social pressure for his strong criticism of the worship of false gods, Jeremiah remained hopeful of God's love and mercies. He knew that God had a plan for his life and that life would not end in emptiness but would continue in rejoicing for eternity.

Jeremiah's hope for the future was based on the new covenant found in the New Testament.

Jeremiah 31:31–33 reads, "Behold, the days come, saith the Lord, that I will make a new covenant with the house of Israel, and with the house of Judah: Not according to the covenant that I made with their fathers in the day that I took them by the hand to bring them out of the land of Egypt; which my covenant they brake, although I was a husband unto them, saith the Lord: But this shall be the covenant that I will make with the house of Israel; After those days, saith the Lord, I will put my law in their inward parts, and write it in their hearts: and will be their God, and they shall be my people."

The new covenant is God's invitation to all of mankind that God is waiting to give to all of mankind eternal life with the indwelling of the Holy Spirit. God's New Covenant will forgive all of man's sins and remember them no more. The penalty for all of man's sin will be paid with the death and resurrection of God's Son, Jesus Christ. All these blessings are available to anyone who believes in God and His saving grace.

John 13:34–35 reads, "A new commandment I give unto you, that ye love one another as I have loved you, that ye also love one another. By this shall all men know that ye are my disciples, if ye have love one to another."

Jesus was the fulfillment of God's love for all of mankind. So now this same love is shared by each believer as a sign to the world.

Life as a Believer

Today, we still have the worship of false gods and the lack of repentance. Jeremiah's life as a messenger was difficult due to the refusal of the people to follow God's commands. God spoke directly to Jeremiah and blessed him. God spoke through Jeremiah to deliver a message of condemnation and hope. These messages were met with anger, hate, and physical harm.

Even though Jeremiah was hated and mistreated, God continued to speak through Jeremiah and protect him. Like Jeremiah, the messages we deliver may not be accepted and may be met with hate and ridicule. However, our Master is the one true God who is the Creator of all and His plan for our life is waiting for us to fulfill. Our understanding of God and His plan for mankind is limited and requires us to place our trust in Him each day to open new doors and provide direction.

We live in a fallen world that is filled with disease, natural disasters, sin, and evil. As Jeremiah, we place our trust in God and His promises.

Jeremiah 29:11–12 reads, "For I know the thoughts that I think toward you, saith the Lord, thoughts of peace, and not of evil, to give you an expected end. Then shall ye call upon me, and ye shall go and pray unto me, and I will hearken unto you."

The Christian loves God and is happy to commune with Him each day in prayer. God is in the thoughts of a Christian's daily life and his life is a sacrifice to his Lord and Savior. His purpose as a Christian is to share God's grace and love to those around him and to lessen the sorrows and pain of a fallen world.

As a prophet, Jeremiah was God's messenger. The messages that he delivered were highly critical of the temple priests and the evil practices that took place in Jerusalem, Judea, and Israel. The worship of idols and other false gods were common practices along with the inability to recognize sin and lack of repentance.

John 14:16–17 reads, "And I will pray the Father, and he shall give you another Comforter, that he may ahide with you for ever; Even the Spirit of truth; whom the world cannot receive, because it seeth him not, neither knoweth him: but ye know him: for he dwelleth with you , and shall be in you."

Jesus Christ is now sitting on the right hand of God in heaven and has now made the power of the Holy Spirit available to all believers. Jesus before ascending into heaven directed the disciples to return to Jerusalem and wait for the gift of the Holy Spirit before going out into the world and teach the gospel.

Today, God's love is still being realized by millions of Christians as they live out their lives directed by the Holy Spirit. Man was created with a physical and spiritual body. The spiritual body of the Christian is eager to welcome and commune with the Holy Spirit. This commune with the Holy Spirit will have a profound effect upon man and cause man to be convicted of his many sins and the evil that he is exposed to. The Holy Spirit will take up residence with the soul and spirit of man and create a bond that cannot be broken.

How God Communicates

The angel of the Lord appeared to Joseph four times in a dream. In the first dream, the angel explained that Joseph should take Mary as his wife due to the fact she was conceived by the Holy Spirit. In the second dream, the angel tells Joseph to take Mary and Jesus and flee to Egypt. In the third dream, the angel tells Joseph to travel to Israel due to the fact those that sought to kill Jesus were no longer living. In the fourth dream, God warns Joseph not to go to Judea, but to remain in Galilee and Nazareth.

Joseph was a righteous man who followed the instructions given to him in the dreams without question.

We are to live a righteous life like Joseph and follow God's instruction without question. In this situation, an angel appeared to Joseph in a number of dreams that detailed instructions as to how, where and when to travel to avoid danger. An angel may appear in our dreams that may instruct us as to how to avoid danger. In other words, an angel may communicate with us through a dream that may result in providing protection.

Before making any decision we need to spend time in prayer asking God for his blessings and direction. One major danger that prevents man from humbling himself in prayer is the ego. Pride has always been one of man's weaknesses and has been responsible for man's many failures throughout history. Pride will destroy the commune between the Holy Spirit and man's soul. Pride is a tenacious sin that will attach itself to man for his entire Christian life.

John 14:26 reads, "But the Comforter, which is the Holy Ghost, whom the Father will send in my name, he shall teach you all things, and bring all things to your remembrance, whatsoever I have said unto you."

The Holy Spirit will teach Christians in a number of different ways. The Holy Spirit will bring to memory the teachings of Jesus Christ and how He conducted His life in the face of many challenges. The Holy Spirit takes on an active role in a Christian life by allowing him to be overwhelmed at times with great joy and at other times with great sorrows.

The Holy Spirit communicates our prayers to God. We are all sinners and are in need of the Holy Spirit's power and wisdom to bridge the vast crevasse that separates man from God. The Holy Spirit will provide us with the words, wisdom and strength to meet any challenge.

Obedience

Throughout Jesus' life He would say, "If you love me you will keep my commandments." The first commandment is that we should love God with all our heart and soul and the second is that we should love our neighbor as we love ourselves.

The baptism of Jesus was an important part of Jesus' ministry and was recognized with God's verbal approval directly from heaven.

Matthew 3:16–17 reads, "And Jesus, when he was baptized, went up straightway out of the water: and, lo, the heavens were opened unto him, and he saw the spirit of God descending like a dove, and lighting upon him: And lo a voice from heaven, saying, This is my beloved Son, in whom I am well pleased."

Jesus lived His life as an example for all of mankind. During Jesus' baptism the heavens opened up and the Spirit of God descended upon Jesus. As the water rushes over your body your soul is renewed. It is at this moment of great joy that your soul is filled with a new life and craves to be united with its' Creator. John the Baptist had firsthand experience as he watched the Holy Spirit descend from heaven and rest upon Jesus the Lamb of God.

John 1:32 reads, "And John bare record, saying, I saw the Spirit descending from heaven like a dove, and it abode upon him."

The Spirit of God descends from heaven and seals the soul of each person forever who is baptized in the name of the Father, Son, and Holy Spirit.

John the Baptist was one of God's messengers. His message was that the Messiah was coming and that it was time to repent of your sins and to be obedient to God's law. Jesus did meet John the Baptist and asked John to baptize Him to fulfill God's will for his life. John was obedient and baptized Jesus.

John the Baptist's father was Zechariah a priest and husband to Elizabeth. Elizabeth was a relative of Mary the mother of Jesus.

Luke 1:13 reads, "But the angel said unto him, Fear not, Zechariah: for thy prayer is heard; and thy wife Elisabeth shall bear thee a son, and thou shalt call his name John."

Luke 1:19 reads, "And the angel answering said unto him, I am Gabriel, that stand in the presence of God; and am sent to speak unto thee, and to show thee these glad tidings."

God was preparing and planning for the baptism of Jesus Christ and the beginning of His ministry.

Jesus appeared to the eleven disciples after his death and spoke of the great commission.

Matthew 28:19–20 reads, "Go ye therefore, and teach all nations, baptizing them in the name of the Father, and of the Son, and of the Holy Ghost; Teaching them to observe all things whatsoever I have commanded you: and , lo, I am with you always, even unto the end of the world, Amen."

God's command to be baptized was initiated with John the Baptist. Jesus followed God's will and was baptized and commanded his disciples to go out and teach all nations, baptizing them in the name of the Father, the Son, and Holy Spirit.

The act of making a decision to become a Christian requires that a person follow God's word and commands. The process begins with admitting that you are a sinner and that you are in need of forgiveness for those sins. This is a lifelong process that requires a great deal of dedication to following God's word.

We begin each day in prayer asking for the strength and wisdom to follow God's word and to be prepared to share God's love with those He brings into our lives.

Peter

PETER (SIMON) THE APOSTLE (1 BC to 64 AD) had one brother Andrew who also became an Apostle and a follower of Jesus the Christ. It is believed Peter wrote the Gospel of Mark with the assistance of John Mark. It is also generally believed he wrote the First and Second Epistle of Peter. He was a fisherman with little formal education, lived in the village of Bethsaida, and worked in Capernaum with fishing nets on the Sea of Galilee. He was married, worked with his father (Jona) and brother, Andrew in a physically demanding job with long hours. Generally, Simon (Peter) was considered to be an out spoken man who felt free to share his opinions and at times a little rough around the edges. The area was considered to be in extreme poverty with a strong sense of independence from Jerusalem.

The first mention of Simon (Peter) is after Jesus is baptized in the Jordan River south of the Sea of Galilee. It appears both Peter and Andrew were both associated with John the Baptist and his ministry. When John the Baptist met Jesus he knew who Jesus was and immediately called Him the Lamb of God. It is also possible that John the Baptist may have been aware of Jesus of Nazareth from relatives and other acquaintances. It should be noted Peter, Andrew and Jesus were about around thirty years of age with Andrew being the youngest.

John 1:35–42 reads, "Again the next day after John stood, and two of his disciples; And looking upon Jesus as he walked, he saith, Behold the Lamb of God! And two disciples heard him speak, and they followed Jesus. And Jesus turned, and saw them following, and saith unto them, "What seek ye?" They said unto him, Rabbi, (which is to say, being interpreted, Master), where dwellest thou? He saith unto them, "Come and see." They came and saw where he dwelt, and abode with him that day: for it was about the tenth hour. One of the two which heard John speak, and followed him, was Andrew, Simon Peter's brother. He first findeth his own brother

Simon, and saith unto him, We have found the Messiah, which is, being interpreted, the Christ. And he brought him to Jesus. And when Jesus beheld him, he said, Thou art Simon the son of Jona, thou shalt be called Cephas, which is by interpretation, A stone."

This first meeting between Peter, Andrew and Jesus resulted in Andrew and Peter deciding to become more involved with the ministry of Jesus of Nazareth. Jesus knew Simon (Peter) and knew that Peter would be a leader for the Apostles and the foundation of Christ's church.

The next time we learn of Simon (Peter) he is in Capernaum or Bethsaida fishing with his partners the sons of Zebedee, John and James.

Luke 5: 1–10 reads, "And it came to pass, that, as the people pressed upon him to hear the word of God, he stood by the lake of Gennesaret. And saw two ships standing by the lake: but the fishermen were gone out of them, and were washing their nets. And he entered into one of the ships, which were Simon's, and prayed him that he would thrust out a little from the land. And he sat down, and taught the people out of the ship. Now when he had left speaking, he said unto Simon, "Launch out into the deep, and let down your nets for a draught." And Simon answering said unto him, Master, we have toiled all night, and have taken nothing: nevertheless at thy word I will let down the net. And when they had this done, they enclosed a great multitude of fishes: and their net brake. And they beckoned unto their partners, which were in the other ship, that they should come and help them. And they came, and filled both ships, so that they began to sink. When Simon Peter saw it, he fell down at Jesus' knees, saying, Depart from me; for I am a sinful man, O Lord. For he was astonished, and all that were with him, at the draught of the fishes which they had taken: And so was also James, and John, the sons of Zebedee, which were partners with Simon. And Jesus said unto Simon, "Fear not; from henceforth thou shalt catch men."

As Peter spent more time with Jesus he became more aware of the sin in his life. As we spend more time in God's word we become more aware of the sin in our lives.

Placing Our Trust in God's Direction

Jesus stepped into Peter's boat due to the crowds of people and asks Peter to take them out a few feet so that He may continue to preach to the people on the shore. Jesus continued His preaching of the gospel as Simon Peter listened. After which, Jesus tells Peter to move his boat out to deeper water and cast his nets. Peter explained he had fished all night and there were no fish to be caught. However, Peter obeys Jesus' wishes and goes out to deeper water and lets down his nets. And, to his surprise he nets so many fish that he asks John and James to bring out their boat to help pull in all the fish. Both boats worked together landing the fish to the point to where both boats began to sink. The reality of the situation hits Peter hard to the point to where he realizes he is in the presence of a miracle and God's messenger. Peter falls at the feet of Jesus and asks that Jesus leave him due to the sin in his life. He feels he is not worthy to be in the presence of Jesus and asks that Jesus depart from him. Satan (fallen man, natural man) is at work with Peter trying to convince him not to follow Jesus because of his sin. Peter physically was a strong man capable of pulling in large heavy nets filled with fish, but spiritually he was weak and was overcome by fear of failure. Jesus knew that Peter would grow to be a great disciple and continued to love him and work with him regardless of his human frailties. God shows that same love and patience today as we wrestle with fear and strive to grow in faith.

Next we find Jesus at Peter's mother-in-law's house. She is sick and needs immediate attention.

Luke 4:38–39 reads, "And he arose out of the synagogue, and entered into Simon's house. And, Simon's wife's mother was taken with a great fever; and they besought him for her. And he stood over her, and rebuked the fever; and it left her: and immediately she arose and ministered unto them."

Peter is present with Jesus as He rebukes the fever and allows Peterʼs wifeʼs mother to continue with her life. As they continue their travels Peterʼs knowledge and understanding of Jesusʼ ministry grows stronger to the point Peter becomes the lead apostle.

Mark 3:13–19 reads, "And he goeth up into a mountain, and calleth unto him whom he would and they came unto him. And he ordained twelve, that they should be with him, and that he might send them forth to preach. And to have power to heal sicknesses, and to cast out devils; And Simon the surnamed Peter; And James the son of Zebedee, and John the brother of James; and he surnamed them Boanerges, which is, the sons of thunder. And Andrew, and Philip, and Bartholomew, and Matthew, and Thomas, and James the son of Alphaeus, and Thaddeus, and Simon the Canaanite, And Judas Iscariot, which also betrayed him: and they went into a house."

Jesus goes to the mountain to pray and make the decision as to who would be ordained to be His disciples. Simon Peter is the first to be considered and the first to be ordained to be one of Jesusʼ disciples. Obviously, Peter is held in high regard as a leader and that Jesus would delegate great responsibility and power to heal the sick and cast out demons. Peter was a follower who was eager to learn and who was quick to assume more responsibility over the next two years.

God had a covenant with the Jewish people and wanted to ensure that they were the first to hear the good news that Jesus was the Messiah. Peter and the disciples first mission was to go out into the Jewish community by twos to preach that Jesus was the Messiah, heal the sick, and cast out demons. Peter leads the disciples as they travel from village to village preaching that Jesus is the Messiah.

As Peter, we are all aware of the present and the lessons given to us from history, but we have no knowledge of the future. However, it is God and His divine direction that makes allowances for future events. The Christian is at peace in the knowledge that God has prepared a place for them.

Understanding and Appreciating God's Power

MARK 5:37–43 READS, "AND he suffered no man to follow him, save Peter, and James, and John the brother of James. And he cometh to the house of the ruler of the synagogue, and seeth the tumult, and them that wept and wailed greatly. And when he was come in, he said unto them, "Why make ye this ado, and weep? The damsel is not dead, but sleepeth." And they laughed him to scron. But when he had put them all out, he taketh the father and the mother of the damsel, and them that were with him, and entereth in where the damsel was lying. And he took the damsel by the hand, and said unto her, "Talitha cumi"; which is, being interpreted, "Damsel", (I say unto thee,) "arise". And straightway the damsel arose, and walked; for she was of the age of twelve years. And they were astonished with a great astonishment. And he charged them straitly that no man shculd know it; and commanded that something should be given her to eat."

Jesus required that Peter, James, and John be present at this miracle for their own enrichment and for a number of other reasons. These Apostles had to experience and realize the full impact that Jesus was God and that God has power over sin, disease, death, and Satan. They were to act as witnesses to Jesus' Transfiguration and later to Jesus' Ascension. There is no limitation to God's power and the Apostles needed to realize that this power was available through faith. The miracles that Jesus completed were in the presence of faith, for building faith and for proclaiming that Jesus was the Messiah.

A transformation took place within Peter that changed him from an outspoken rough man of thunder, to a humble obedient servant of the Lord God Almighty even to death. He rejoiced the day of his death that he would now be reunited with his Savior that had been crucified over 30 years prior.

Matthew 16:13–16 reads, "When Jesus came into the coasts of Caesarea Philippi, he asked his disciples, saying, "Whom do men say that I the Son of man am?" And they said, Some say that thou art John the Baptist: some, Elijah; and others, Jeremiah, or one of the prophets. He saith unto them, "But whom say ye that I am?" And Simon Peter answered and said, Thou art the Christ, the Son of the living God. And Jesus answered and said unto him, "Blessed art thou, Simon Bar-jona: for flesh and blood hath not revealed it unto thee, but my Father which is in heaven. And I say also unto thee, That thou art Peter, and upon this rock I will build my church; and the gates of hell shall not prevail against it. And I will give unto thee the keys of the kingdom of heaven: and whatsoever thou shalt bind on earth shall be bond in heaven: and whatsoever thou shalt loose on earth shall be loosed in heaven."

Caesarea Philippi is a city located about 120 miles northeast of Jerusalem at the foot of Mount Hermon. The location provides a contrast between Jesus the Messiah and the local culture that is buried in the superstition and acts of pure evil related to the worship of many gods. Herod the Great built a temple near the Mount to celebrate Caesar Augustus, hence the name Caesarea Philippi. Jesus takes the Apostles on the twenty five mile journey from Galilee to Caesarea Philippi for the purpose of allowing them to be free of the daily distractions and to concentrate on their mission with Jesus. When Jesus asked the question, "But whom say ye that I am?" It is only Peter that responses without hesitation and said, Thou art the Christ, the Son of the living God. It was Peter that reached that level of spiritual discernment and allowed him to freely identify Jesus' deity as being God's Son.

God blessed Peter throughout his life for his faith, for his discernment, and for his unwavering faithfulness. It was Peter and his testimony that God used as the rock that lead the disciples and provided a foundation for the church. Jesus is the Messiah and through Him God is keeping His promise to provide a Savior for all of mankind. God at this point is giving Peter more responsibility and authority for building the church.

God Will Change a Man's Character

ROMAN RULE OVER ISRAEL was severe and the penalty for a convicted criminal was death on a cross. The convicted criminal was required to carry their cross to the place of crucifixion. This was a long and painful death that may last three or four days. To the common man at that time the cross meant only one thing, a long and painful death. Peter may have thought Jesus was there to rescue them from this oppressive Roman rule and become King of Israel.

Consequently, when Peter heard Jesus explain he was going to die and rise on the third day he was bewildered. Peter was a bold and impetuous Apostle who did not hesitate to challenge Jesus when he spoke of His own death.

Matthew 16:22–23 reads, "Then Peter took Him, and began to rebuke him, saying, Be it far from thee, Lord: this shall and be unto thee. But he turned, and said unto Peter, "Get thee behind me, Satan: thou art an offense unto me: for thou savorest not the things that be of God, thou those that be of men."

Peter's reaction reveals that he did not fully understand the purpose for Jesus' death and resurrection. Peter is going through a transformation from a natural man with many frailties to a spiritual man. Jesus sees that Satan is once again trying to prevent Him from carrying out God's promise to provide salvation for all of mankind. Jesus was also teaching that there is a cost related to discipleship and that cost may involve losing your life.

Matthew 16:24 reads, Then said Jesus unto his disciples, "If any man will come after me, let him deny himself, and take up his cross, and follow me."

Jesus was telling his Apostles that they need to realize that there is a cost related to following Him. Peter and the Apostles were learning that following Jesus would involve a cost and part of that cost would be to deny self.

Jesus, Peter, and the Apostles traveled to Jerusalem where the final days unfolded for Jesus' life.

Matthew 26:40 reads, "And he cometh unto the disciples, and findeth them asleep, and saith unto Peter, What, could ye not watch with me one hour?"

Gethsemane was a beautiful garden on the slopes of the Mount of Olives that was used as a place for rest and reflection. It was a perfect place for Jesus, Peter, and the disciples to pray. Peter and the disciples again showed their human weakness when Jesus finds them sleeping rather than praying. Even during this final hour of greatest need, Peter fails to keep watch and pray.

During this late hour of darkness Judas, Malchus (servant of the high priest), and a number of the soldiers slithered into the gardens to betray and arrest Jesus.

John 18:10 reads, "Then Simon Peter having a sword drew it, and smote the high priest's servant, and cut off his right ear. The servant's name was Malchus."

Peter again was quick to react and was willing to defend Jesus with his sword. He was highly capable physically and knew how to defend himself and Jesus with a sword. Peter was capable of being very loyal to Jesus, but at times was rash and hasty. It seems his formal training was limited and he did make mistakes at times, but he did assume responsibility readily and did have natural leadership skills. One of Peter's greatest failures was when he denies Jesus three times.

Peter's transformation to a follower of Jesus was not without issues due to many different personality characteristics. However, Peter's strong commitment and faithfulness to Jesus overcame any personality issues. We often meet people with personalities that are not inviting or we find abrasive. Peter may have been a person that we found to be abrasive, but God used him in a mighty way.

We do not fully understand God's plans and methods for directing our lives. However, we continue to move ahead each day in prayer trusting in God and His grace and blessings.

2 Corinthians 5:17 reads, "Therefore if any man be in Christ, he is a new creature: old things are passed away; behold, all things are become new."

Nothing Is Impossible for God

Peter was present as the high priest began to question Jesus at the palace. Peter sat with the servants so as not to be detected and to listen and watch the hearing conducted by the Sanhedrin. The witnesses against Jesus were for the most part conflicting and not enough to convict Jesus of any crime. However, the high priest began to ask Jesus if he was the Christ the Son of the Blessed. Until this point Jesus had said nothing.

Mark 14: 62 reads, "And Jesus said, I am: and ye shall see the Son of man sitting on the right hand of power, and coming in the clouds of heaven."

Jesus in this statement provides the information that is needed to convict him of blasphemy and the death penalty. Peter was listening intently and must have been completely demoralized when he heard Jesus speak and the sentence of death that was issued. Peter could no longer protect his Savior with his might and sword. Fear (Satan) took hold and Peter tried to hide in the crowds, however, he was spotted and questioned a few times if he was a follower of Jesus. His desire to survive overtook him and he lied when he said he did not know Jesus three times before the cock crowed twice. At that moment in time Peter recalled what Jesus had said and he left and wept bitterly.

After the crucifixion, Peter and the other disciples were in great distress and in hiding not sure if they would be next. Mary Magdalene was the first at the grave site in the early morning hours.

John 20:1–7 reads, "The first day of the week cometh Mary Magdalene early, when it was yet dark, unto the sepulcher, and seeth the stone taken away from the sepulcher. Then she runneth, and cometh to Simon Peter, and to the other disciple, whom Jesus loved, and said unto them, They have taken away the Lord out of the sepulcher, and we know not where they have laid him. Peter therefore went forth, and that other disciple, and came to the sepulcher. So they ran both together: and the other disciples did outrun Peter, and came first to the sepulcher. And he stooping down, and looking in, saw the linen clothes lying; yet went he not in. Then cometh Simon Peter following him, and went into the sepulcher, and seeth the linen clothes lie. And the napkin, that was about his head, not lying with the linen clothes, but wrapped together in a place by itself."

Peter as head of the church and beloved of God was the first to see the risen Lord and Savior. Jesus' second appearance was in a locked room with the eleven disciples.

Luke 24:36–43 reads, "And as they thus spake, Jesus himself stood in the midst of them, and saith unto them, Peace be unto you. But they were terrified and affrighted, and supposed that they had seen a spirit. And he said unto them, Why are ye troubled? and why do thoughts arise in your hearts? Behold my hands and my feet, that it is I myself: handle me, and see; for a spirit hath not flesh and bones, as ye see me have. And when he had thus spoken, he showed them his hands and his feet. And while they yet believed not for joy, and wondered, he said unto them, Have ye here any meat. And they gave him a piece of a broiled fish, and of a honeycomb. And he took it, and did eat before them."

Jesus' second appearance was before his eleven Apostles in a room that had been locked from the inside. In a moment Jesus appeared standing before his disciples in a body that appeared as any other with both skin and bones. In fact, He invited his disciples to examine his hands and feet to verify that it was his body that was crucified on the cross. He also ate fish and honey. This appearance by Jesus in front of his disciples gave them no room for doubt that Jesus had died and then rose from the grave. It was God's grace that allowed for the repentance and remission of sin for all of mankind. Peter and all the disciples were at this time commissioned by God to preach the saving grace of Jesus beginning with Jerusalem and then all the nations.

Nothing is impossible for God. Jesus was crucified, died and then appeared before His disciples.

God's Requirements

PETER AND THE APOSTLES were given the Holy Spirit to continue the work of Jesus and the preaching of the good news that Jesus had risen and had defeated death for all of mankind. The disciples were now preaching that Jesus was the ultimate sacrifice for all man's sin. The church and its' people may now receive the forgiveness of their sins by believing in the death and resurrection of Jesus, God's only Son. The sacrifice of God's Son forgave the sins of all mankind from the past, present and future.

John 20: 21–23 reads, "Then said Jesus to them again, Peace be unto you: as my Father hath sent me, even so send I you. And when he had said this, he breathed on them, and saith unto them, Receive ye the Holy Ghost: Whosoever sins ye remit, they are remitted unto them, and whosesoever sins ye retain, they are retained."

Peter had failed and denied he knew Jesus three times after Jesus was found guilty of blasphemy and was sentenced to death. Jesus, after His resurrection confronts Peter three times with the same question.

John 21:15–17 reads, "So when they had dined, Jesus saith to Simon Peter, "Simon son of Jonah, lovest thou me more than these? He said unto him, Yea, Lord; you knowest that I love thee. He saith unto him, Feed my lambs. He said to him again the second time, Simon, son of Jonah, lovest thou me? He said unto him, Yea, Lord; thou knowest that I love thee. He saith unto him, Feed my sheep. He saith unto him the third time, Simon, son of Jonah, lovest thou me? Peter was grieved because he said unto him the third time, Lovest thou me? And he said unto him, Lord, thou knowest all things: thou knowest that I love thee. Jesus saith unto him, Feed my sheep."

Peter was confronted by Jesus asking him if he loved his Savior, Jesus. The questions by Jesus and the answers by Peter were heard by all and there was now no doubt that Peter has confirmed and committed to completing his mission to preach the gospel. Peter, the head of the church and commissioned by God still failed and still had lapses in judgment. Peter's journey and all of mans journeys are not without daily challenges due to the old natural man and Satan. However, God does not fail us, His grace and forgiveness is never ending and is available to all those who repent.

Jesus' challenge to Peter is that if he loves Him he needs to feed His sheep. It is not uncommon for sheep to wander while they are grazing and will at times get lost. They have no sense of direction and if they become lost they cannot find their way back to the flock. Man has no sense of spiritual direction and if he becomes lost he needs someone to help him find his way back to his Master and Lord. Sheep are completely defenseless, without sharp teeth, sharp claws, or the speed to escape an attack from a wolf or mountain lion. It is important for sheep to stay close to their shepherd for protection. The same is true for man. Man needs to stay close to God on a daily basis to be able to consume spiritual food and water to maintain enough strength to withstand the attacks from Satan and his demons.

Jesus was not only commanding Peter to feed his sheep and the church, but to maintain a close daily relationship with God that would provide the strength to withstand the relentless attacks from Satan and his demons. Man has a soul that is completely dependent on spiritual nourishment. This nourishment comes from only one source and that one source is God that transforms the soul in daily prayer and study.

Peter at this point was growing in strength and power as the Holy Spirit took on a greater role in his life. Peter's message to the people of Jerusalem had a huge impact and many believed in the message of the cross.

Christians are commanded to feed God's sheep. Some are commanded to travel to the outer parts of the world and preach the good news that God has prepared a place in heaven for those who believe in Jesus.

Do Not Underestimate God's Holy Spirit

THE HOLY SPIRIT ON the day of Pentacost filled Peter and caused him to deliver a message so strong that it converted over 3,000 people to the belief in Jesus Christ as the risen Savior for all of mankind. Peter spoke of the fulfillment of the prophecy that Jesus would come to be the sacrifice for all of man's sins, that his works and His resurrection would attest that He was the Messiah. He was condemned and crucified by Jewish and Roman Courts for confessing to the truth that He was the Messiah. He was ascended into heaven to sit at God's right hand and has now sent the Holy Spirit to direct and strengthen our spirits. Jesus our glorified Messiah has poured forth the Holy Spirit. We pray today for the out pouring of the Holy Spirit for the spiritual conversions of millions of people whose spirit is either consumed by self or lost to the desire of money and power.

Peter's spirit and spiritual life was growing in strength to the point of allowing the Holy Spirit to perform miracles through him.

Acts 9:39–43 reads, "Then Peter arose and went with them. When he was come, they brought him into the upper chamber: and all the widows stood by him weeping, and showing the coats and garments which Dorcas made, while she was with them. But Peter put them all forth, and kneeled down, and prayed; and turning him to the body said, Tabitha, arise. And she opened her eyes, and when she saw Peter, she sat up. And he gave her his hand, and lifted her up, and when he has called the saints and widows, presented her alive. And it was known throughout all Joppa; and many believed in the Lord. And it came to pass, that he tarried many days in Joppa with one Simon a tanner."

This first and most powerful miracle performed by an Apostle was completed by Peter. This miracle further confirmed Peter's position as leader of the Apostles. In addition, Peter spent some time in Joppa with Simon the tanner, preaching and teaching to both Jews and Gentiles.

The second miracle related to Peter was the conversion of a Gentile, a Roman centurion. Peter was contacted by Cornelius, a centurion living in Caesarea a city located north of Joppa on the Mediterranean Sea. Cornelius was visited by an angel who told him to contact Peter. So Cornelius summoned Peter to come to Caesarea.

Acts 10:25–28 reads, "And as Peter was coming in, Cornelius met him, and fell down at his feet, and worshiped him. But Peter took him up, saying, Stand up: I myself also am a man. And as he talked with him, he went in, and found many that were come together. And he said unto them, Ye know how that it is an unlawful thing for a man that is a Jew to keep company, or come unto one of another nation; but God hath showed me that I should not call any man common or unclean."

Peter again realized with God's assistance that God was no respecter of people. There is no place in Christianity for prejudice against another man regardless if he is a Gentile or Jew. God accepts all men from all nations who believe in Him, love Him, and obey Him.

Peter's words were revolutionary and moved the church into the worldwide mission of providing the saving Grace in the faith of the Lord Jesus Christ. The Holy Spirit came upon all that heard Peter's message and believed. All men are equal in God's sight. It is man's decision to either accept judgment or salvation. Salvation is faith that is based on the belief on the risen Savior, Jesus Christ, God's only Son.

As Peter's reputation began to grow; so did resentment grow among the Jews and the Romans against the early church.

Christians need to be open to all men they encounter and realize that nothing is impossible with God. However, do not remain in a place where God's words are not accepted. Shake the dust off your feet and move on.

God Uses Many Different Methods

KING HEROD AGRIPPA 1 was under pressure due to a famine and decided to blame the church for Israel's problems. King Agrippa 1 was aware of the Jewish resentment of the early Christian church and took advantage of every opportunity to curry favor of the Jews. In this case, the King found that it pleased the Jews when he executed James (son of Zebedee and brother of John) with a sword, so Herod imprisoned Peter. A public trial would allow all the Jews to express their hatred for the early Christian church and increase Herod's status in Jerusalem.

Acts 12: 1–3 reads, "Now about that time Herod the King stretched forth his hands to vex certain of the church. And he killed James the brother of John with the sword. And because he saw it pleased the Jews, he proceeded further to take Peter also. Then were the days of unleavened bread."

Peter was placed in chains and under heavy guard twenty four hours a day.

Acts 12:7–8 reads, "And, behold, the angel of the Lord came upon him, and a light shinned in the prison: and he smote Peter on the side, and raised him up, saying, Arise up quickly, And his chains fell from his hands. And the angel said unto him, Gird thyself, and bind on thy sandals. And so he did. And he saith unto him, Cast thy garment about thee, and follow me."

Even though Peter was under heavy guard and in chains, they were not enough to prevent God from freeing Peter from this prison. It was God's angel that took the chains from Peter, prevented the guards from acting, and opened the gates without keys. Peter was free from certain death and returned to the house of Mary (John Mark's house). The first response from the household was it must be Peter's angel. Peter told the household to tell James (Jesus half brother) what had transpired and that he was free. Peter left the area and began his ministry possibly to Asia Minor.

The Apostle Peter also encountered some conflict when he traveled to Antioch where he was confronted by Paul for not eating with the Gentiles.

Galatians 2:11–13 reads, "But when Peter was come to Antioch, I withstood him to the face, because he was to be blamed. For before that certain came from James, he did eat with the Gentiles: but when they were came, he withdrew and separated himself, fearing them which were of the circumcision. And the other Jews dissembled likewise with him; insomuch that Barnabas also was carried away with their dissimulation."

Again, God is patience with Peter as he tried to understand the relationship between the Jew and Gentile. Peter a Jew, was struggling with following Jewish law and at the same time did not want to offend the Gentiles and Paul a Roman by birth. Paul and the Gentiles were not bound by Jewish law and were equal to all men in God's eye.

Galatians 2:16 reads, "Knowing that a man is not justified by the works of the law, but by the faith of Jesus Christ, even we have believed in Jesus Christ, that we might be justified by the faith of Christ, and not by works of the law: for by the works of the law shall no flesh be justified."

Again, God reminds Peter that his salvation is only possible by the atoning death of his only Son. A believer in Jesus Christ lives a life that glorifies God by obeying, serving, and praising God for his countless blessings. Salvation cannot be achieved by performing good works or by obeying the Jewish law. Salvation is only possible by believing in the death and resurrection of God's only Son, the Lord Jesus Christ.

God has power over all things and can control all people and all activity within the universe. All things are possible with God. Prayer is talking with God and is extremely important. It is more than just asking for things but includes confession of sins, thanksgiving, and praise. 1 John 3:22 reads, "And whatsoever we ask, we receive of him, because we keep his commandments, and do those things that are pleasing in his sight."

Trusting God and Obeying His Word

GOD LOVED PETER REGARDLESS of his many human frailties and failures. God took Peter a fisherman from Galilee with little formal education and built the Christian church with the Apostle. God was extremely patient with Peter even though he denied Christ three times and struggled in understanding God's direction for his life. Peter was the first Apostle to recognize Jesus as the Messiah, the first to take on the commitment to full service, and the first to lead the Apostles in forming the church. His single purpose in life was to please God, preach the gospel, serve the poor, and to lead the Apostles. The Holy Spirit over took Peter in a great way that allowed him to perform miracles, to preach a message that saved the souls of over three thousand in one meeting, and to direct the Apostles in forming the church. Peter was truly a unique individual that lived for his Savior and devoted a hundred percent of his life to saving souls.

The Jewish culture was deeply rooted in following the Jewish leadership and obeying Jewish law. Any deviation from the Jewish law was strongly discouraged and could result in stoning. King Herod and the Roman government were constantly looking for any signs of trouble within the local Jewish community for fear of a revolt against their ruthless control. When Herod learned he would gain favor for killing James, he started an effort to punish the Apostles and jailed Peter. Herod's plan was to jail Peter and place him on display in a public trial. This would both allow the Jews to air their hatred of the Apostles and for Herod to build a good reputation among the Jews. Peter and the Apostles were forced to avoid both the Jewish and Roman leadership to prevent persecution and to stay alive.

Peter traveled to Antioch (ruins lie near Antakya, Turkey) where Christianity grew in popularity. Antioch is also known as the Cradle of Christianity.

It is believed Peter then traveled to Rome where he worked in forming the early Christian church in Rome. It is believed this was also during the time of Nero and the great fire that consumed most of Rome. Emperor Nero placed the blame for the fire on the Christians in the city and looked to jail Peter and have him put to death. The Apostle Peter in 64AD elected to be crucified upside down, since he felt he was not worthy to be crucified in the same manner as Jesus his Savior.

John 21: 5–7 reads, "Then Jesus saith unto them, children have ye any meat? They answered him, No. And he saith unto them, Cast the net on the right side of the ship, and ye shall find. They cast therefore, and now they were not able to draw it for the multitude of fishes. Therefore that disciple whom Jesus loved saith unto Peter, It is the Lord. Now when Simon Peter heard that it was the Lord, he girt his fisher's coat unto him, for he was naked, and did cast himself into the sea."

We often find ourselves in situations where we do not have the answer and we realize only God could solve the problem. As Peter, we may have been fishing for a great deal of time in the wrong location. So, when God makes a request we need to be open to His direction.

Philippians 4, 6–7 reads, " Be careful for nothing: but in every thing by prayer and supplication with thanksgiving let your requests be made known unto God. And the peace of God, which passeth all understanding, shall keep your hearts and minds through Christ Jesus."

We should enter each situation in prayer asking for God's direction and understanding. We should be careful not to rely on our own skills but to review each step to ensure we are following God's direction and will. Obviously, we should reject any action that is not in agreement with God's law and statutes. The Ten Commandments are straight forward and leaves little for interpretation. However, God's statutes and ordinances cover many areas and require a common sense approach for application. The statutes cover generosity, slavery, bribery and corruption, laws and courts, using authority, justice and many more topics.

Trusting in God's Power

The Apostle Peter at one point asked a question about the Apostle John and his future. Jesus basically tells Apostle Peter that it is not any of his concern and that he should concentrate on following Jesus' direction.

John 21: 20–23 reads, "Then Peter, turning about, seeth the disciple whom Jesus loved following; which also leaned on his bread at supper, and said, Lord, which is he that betrayeth thee? Peter seeing him saith to Jesus, Lord, and what shall this man do? Jesus saith unto him, If I will that he tarry till I come, what is that to thee? Follow thou me."

Jesus at this point gives some indication that he may have special plans for the Apostle John and his future mission. The Apostle John did live out his life to the age of ninety four at the Church of Ephesus where he continued his work preaching and writing.

The Apostle John confirms that he can testify of these facts since he was physically present with Jesus as he preached, healed the weak and died on the cross to provide all of mankind a path to salvation.

John 21:24 reads, "This is the disciple which testifieth of these things, and wrote these things: and we know that his testimony is true."

The Holy Bible only records a small portion of all that was spoken by Jesus and the many acts of passion He completed. The Apostle John guided by the Holy Spirit recorded all that needed to be transcribed and to be included in the Holy Bible.

The Apostle John was part of the inner circle of Disciples that received personal instruction from Jesus as he raised people from the dead, healed people from many different illnesses and provided the way of salvation.

Mark 5:37–40 reads, "And he suffered no man to follow him, save Peter, and James, and John the brother of James. And he cometh to the house of the ruler of the synagogue, and seeth the tumult, and them that wept and wailed greatly. And when he was come in, he saith unto them, Why make ye this ado, and weep? The damsel is not dead, but sleepeth. And they laughed him to scorn. But when he had put them all out, he taketh the father and the mother of the damsel, and them that were with him, and entereth in where the damsel was lying."

Jesus instructs John, Peter, and James that those that are disruptive, negative, and faithless need to be removed from the area. Jesus at this time purged the room, the house, and the premises of all the people that were laughing him to scorn. Our thoughts, deeds, and emotions are either righteous or sinful. People are either in the light or in the darkness. In this case, sin and Satan were in control of these people that were laughing. Each day we need to be aware of our speech, thoughts, and emotions to ensure they are not sinful.

Jesus was teaching the Apostle Peter and others you should not proceed until the area is clean of sin and those that are present are believers. This powerful and miraculous miracle occurred when Jesus was in complete control. We struggle with righteousness and sin throughout the day as we entertain ideas and thoughts, consider actions to take, and decide on language to use which was also present in the Upper Room and in the Garden of Gethsemane. It was late when the disciples left the last supper and walked through the dark streets of Jerusalem on their way to the Mount of Olives. The Apostle John had no idea that the information he just received about the betrayal from Jesus would transpire within hours at the Garden of Gethsemane. Jesus continued to teach and prepare his disciples about His betrayal, death and resurrection.

God has given us the Holy Spirit who communes and instructs us throughout each and every day. The Holy Spirit will convict us of sin that is in our lives. However, a person that is dead in their transgressions has broken that relationship with the Holy Spirit and they will not be convicted by their sin. A person that has denied Jesus and has refused to invite Jesus into their life will not experience the communion of the Holy Spirit.

God Instructed Us How to Pray

The Apostle Peter and the other disciples continued to walk in the dark to the Garden of Gethsemane where Jesus prayed. It was the Apostle John who listened with great care to record Jesus' prayer.

John 17: 1–26 reads, "These words spake Jesus, and lifted up his eyes to heaven, and said, "Father, the hour is come; glorify thy Son, that thy Son also may glorify thee. As thou hast given him power over all flesh, that he should give eternal life to as many as thou hast given him. And this is life eternal, that they might know thee the only true God, and Jesus Christ, whom thou hast sent. I have glorified thee on the earth: I have finished the work which thou gavest me to do. And now, O Father, glorify thou me with thine own self with the glory which I had with thee before the world was. I have manifested thy name unto the men which thou gavest me out of the world: thine they were, and thou gavest them me: and they have kept thy word. Now they have know that all things whatsoever thou hast given me are of thee. For I have given unto them the words which thou gavest me; and they have received them, and have known surely that I came out from thee, and they have believed that thou didst send me. I pray for them: I pray not for the world, but for them which thou hast given me; for they are thine. And all mine are thine, and thine are mine; and I am glorified in them. And now I am no more in the world, but these are in the world, and I come to thee. Holy Father, keep through thine own name those whom thou hast given me, that they may be one, as we are. While I was with them in the world, I kept them in thy name: those that thou gavest me I have kept, and none of them is lost, but the son of perdition; that the scripture might be fulfilled. And now come I to thee; and these things I speak to the world, that they might have my joy fulfilled in themselves. I have given them thy word; and the world hath hated them, because they are not of the world, even as I am not of the world. I pray not that thou shouldest take them out of the world, but that shouldest keep them from evil. They are not of the world, even as I am not of the world. Sanctity them through thy truth; thy word is truth. As thou hast sent me into the world, even so have I also sent them into the world. And for their sakes I sanctify myself, that they also might be sanctified through the truth. Neither pray I for these alone, but for them also which shall believe on me through their word: That they all may be one; as thou, Father, art in me, and I in thee, that they also may be one in us: that the world may believe that thou hast sent me. And the glory which thou gavest me I have given them; that they may be one, even as we are one: I in them, and thou in me, that they may be made perfect in one; and that the world may know that thou hast sent me, and hast loved them, as thou hast loved me. Father, I will that they also, whom thou hast given me, be with me where I am; that they may behold my glory, which thou hast given me: for thou lovedst, me before the foundation of the world. O righteous Father, the world hath not know thee: but I have know thee, and these have know that thou hast sent me. And I have declared unto them thy name, and will declare it: that the love wherewith thou hast loved me may be in them, and I in them."

The Apostle Peter and others were in the Garden of Gethsemane with Jesus when He prayed. Jesus' prayer was to glorify God, and to benefit those present (His Apostles) and for future generations. Jesus prayed that his work was complete here on earth and that He was resting in God's will and His return to the realm of eternity.

The chief purpose of man is to glorify God. As we pray each day we begin by praising God for His sacrifice and for the gift of eternal life. Jesus glorified God by allowing God's power, wisdom, and love be known by man.

God the Gardener

God at times works like a gardener when he trims away those that do not bear fruit, those that are a distraction, and those that spread misinformation.

John 15: 1–7 reads, "I am the true vine, and my Father is the husbandman. Every branch in me that beareth not fruit he taketh away; and every branch that beareth fruit, he purgeth it, that it may bring forth more fruit. Now ye are clean through the word which I have spoken unto you. Abide in me, and I in you. As the branch cannot bear fruit of itself, except it abide in the vine: no more can ye, except ye abide in me. I am the vine, ye are the branches: He that abideth in me, and I in him, the same bringeth forth much fruit: for without me ye can do nothing. If a man abide not in me, he is cast forth as a branch, and is withered; and men gather them, and cast them into fire, and they are burned. If ye abide in me, and my words abide in you, ye shall ask what ye will, and it shall be done unto you."

Jesus explained to the Apostles that they were to preach the gospel and to allow the Holy Spirit to save souls. He also explains that as their understanding becomes more complete and their testimony becomes more effective He would become more involved in their lives. Jesus their Lord through the Holy Spirit guided them, he corrected them, and he open new paths for them to follow.

Jesus also prayed for the Apostles and their faith, knowledge, love, and the indwelling of the Holy Spirit. As the Son of God, Jesus verifies that His Apostles were no longer part of the world. He prayed for those that will become believers by hearing the words spoken by His Apostles.

Jesus' prayer also included a request from the Son to the Father for glory to be given out so that all that hear and see may be blessed. This glory is based on the manifestation of God's gracious love of the Father for the Son and for all of mankind.

The Son was glorified by the Father by giving him authority over all of man's weaknesses. The Son glorified the Father by giving eternal life to all those who believed in the Lord Jesus Christ.

It is believed that some of the Apostles continued to live in Jerusalem for a number of years even after the Crucifixion and Resurrection of Jesus. In about 36 AD, the persecution of Christians continued with Stephen being stoned to death for preaching the gospel. The persecution continued as the Apostle James was executed in about 44AD by King Agrippa. The Apostle John experienced a great loss with the death of his brother James and now the danger was too great for his family to live in the Promised Land settled by the twelve tribes of Judah. John rose to a position of prominence in the Christian Church and was able to move before the destruction of Jerusalem in 70AD by the Romans.

Sometime after this continued persecution of Christians the Apostles started moving to others areas outside of Israel. At this time it is believed the Apostle John moved his family (including the Mother of Jesus) to Ephesus of Asia (Turkey). He was able to move his family away from immediate danger and help spread the gospel to the West. The Apostle John continued his preaching for a number of years and worked with the Apostle Paul, the Apostle Peter, the Apostle Timothy and others in spreading the gospel throughout Asia and West to Europe. Ephesus was known as a city of learning where Christians such as the Apostle John and the Apostle Paul were able to preach the gospel to crowds gathered in the lecture halls. The ministry grew as more people witnessed the healing power of the Holy Spirit and those that were released from demons.

The Apostle Peter's letters to the early church provided some information about the relationship between early believers and the government. Generally speaking, Christians should follow the laws and rules established by the government.

God Empowered Peter

The Apostle Peter was part of the inner circle and leader of the Apostles. Peter was the Apostle that first realized who Jesus was and was anxious to make that confirmation with Jesus and the other disciples.

Matthew 16:16 reads, "And Simon Peter answered and said, Thou art the Christ, the son of the living God."

Jesus acknowledged Peter as a person that would have a major impact on building the church and would be empowered by the Holy Spirit to heal and convert both Jews and Gentiles. The church would grow in numbers as the Apostle Peter and the other Apostles continued to preach the news that Jesus was the Messiah and that their salvation is free if only they believed.

Matthew 16:18–19 reads, "And I say also unto thee, That thou art Peter, and upon this rock I will build my church; and the gates of hell shall not prevail against it. And I will give unto thee the keys of the kingdom of heaven: and whatsoever thou shalt bind on earth shall be bound in heaven: and whatsoever thou shalt loose on earth shalt be loosed in heaven."

Jesus gave the Apostle Peter the keys to heaven. It was at the Day of Pentecost when the Apostle Peter first opened the door to heaven when he began to preach. The Apostle Peter was filled with the Holy Spirit and with God's authority when he began to share God's will for man and how salvation was available for all. Many that heard the Apostle's Peter's words that day believed and allowed the Holy Spirit to enter into their lives. The Apostle Peter had the privilege to announce to those who believed in the Lord Jesus Christ that their sins were forgiven and that the doors to heaven were open for them.

Matthew 16:21–22 reads, "From that time forth began Jesus to show unto his disciples, how that he must go unto Jerusalem, and suffer many things of the elders and chief priests and scribes, and be killed, and be raised again the third day. Then Peter took him, and began to rebuke him, saying, Be it far from thee, Lord: this shall not be unto thee."

Jesus had given the Apostles by this time the faith to withstand the pain and suffering that they would endure as their Savior and Lord was crucified. However, the Apostle Peter was distressed to hear this and did not understand why Jesus' death needed to take place.

Jesus had transformed Peter from a poorly educated man with few skills as a preacher to a man with great courage and faithfulness. He became part of the inner circle of Jesus' Apostles and was present during the Transfiguration. He achieved greatness within the church and held a special position. He began as a man with very humble beginnings and was able to achieve a special position within the church because of his solid rock faith in the Lord Jesus the Christ.

Peter was headstrong and would tell people what to do. He even attempted to tell Jesus what to do. He made many mistakes and was often impetuous and would talk before thinking. He denied Christ three times, he cut off the ear of the high priest's guard, and fell asleep in the garden as Jesus prayed.

However, Peter was also blessed by Jesus and was given the authority to heal and complete miracles. He was able to cast out demons and people were healed simply by believing and being in his presence.

Acts 9: 40–43 reads, "But Peter put them all forth, and kneeled down, and prayed; and turning him to the body said, Tabitha, arise. And she opened her eyes: and when she saw Peter, she sat up. And he gave her his hand, and lifted her up, and when had called the saints and widows, presented her alive. And it was known throughout all Joppa; and many believed in the Lord. And it came to pass, that he tarred many days in Joppa with Simon a tanner."

God is the potter and we are the clay. God walks with us as He allows many of life's experiences to mold us into unique creatures of God.

Repentance is the Beginning

REPENTANCE IS A PROCESS of changing the way we think about a certain issue. A change in the way we think about something leads to a change in attitude, that leads to a change in the way we feel about something, that leads to a change in values and a change in the way we live our lives. Believing in God, believing in God's gift, Jesus Christ and allowing the Holy Spirit to take control of our thoughts and feelings places us in a position of communion with our creator.

Peter's denial of Christ haunted him and caused him to fall into complete repentance when Jesus asked him three times if he loved him. This reaffirmation allowed Peter to move from a fearful man to a man of great maturity and courage. In a state of complete commitment he was able to grow in faith and benefit from a closer walk with his Lord and Savior. Peter's faith in Jesus was responsible for making a dramatic change in Peter from a fisherman to a great leader of the Christian church.

The Apostle Peter and the other Apostles were under pressure by the Roman and Jewish leadership for establishing a church that would challenge their own interests for both financial control and the leadership of the people. The Apostle Peter was eventually jailed and sentenced to death. He asked to be crucified upside down because he felt he was not worthy to be crucified in the same manner as his Lord.

We need to learn from The Apostle Peter and ask ourselves are we living a completely committed life that glorifies our Lord and Savior. As The Apostle Peter, we need to learn from our mistakes, grow in maturity, and become more courageous in our walk and in our ministry. We all make mistakes and we need to spend time in prayer to ask for forgiveness. God will transform us through the study of His word, allowing the Holy Spirit to speak to us, and to take time to recognize how the Holy Spirit works both in our lives and in the lives of others.

It was the Apostle Peter who recognized Jesus first at Galilee and could not wait for the boat and jumped into the sea to meet Jesus. It was the Apostle Peter who was the first to acknowledge Jesus as the Messiah. It was the Apostle Peter who quickly drew his sword to defend Jesus in the Garden of Gethsemane. And, it was God who sent an Angel to release the Apostle Peter from prison.

Acts 12:11 reads, "And when Peter was come to himself, he said, Now I know of a surely, that the Lord hath sent his angel, and hath delivered me out of the hand of Herod, and from all the expectation of the people of the Jews."

If you would like to spend eternity in Heaven with God you need to recognize that you are a sinner and repent of your many sins. Surveys conducted generally conclude that fewer people believe in God and fewer people connect a belief in God with being moral and having good values.

Obviously, the need is great and reversing the trend of fewer believers in God and maintaining a moral standard is extremely challenging. So when Jesus told Peter to feed my sheep he was aware of the great need to teach people of the need to confess their sin and to believe in God the father, Jesus Christ the Son, and the Holy Spirit. Hundreds of millions of people will not spend eternity in heaven with their Creator if they do not confess Jesus as their Lord and turn away from their sins.

Shipwreck

In about 57 AD the Apostle Paul was arrested for breaking Jewish law. He was accused of defiling the temple by bringing Gentiles into it and for not teaching the laws of Moses. Later, Paul did exercise his rights as a Roman citizen and asked that he be allowed to appeal to Caesar. The Apostle Paul accompanied by a centurion was placed in chains and was transported from Caesarea to Rome by ship. The ship with 276 passengers was caught in a storm and was blown off course by six hundred miles over a two week time period that ended in a shipwreck on the island of Malta. All 276 passengers survived the storm.

Acts 27:21–23 reads, "But after a long abstinence Paul stood forth in the midst of them, and said, Sirs, ye should have hearkened unto me, and not have loosed from Crete, and to have gained this harm and loss. And now I exhort you to be of good cheer: for there shall be no loss of any man's life among you, but of the ship. For there stood by me this night the angel of God, whose I am, and whom I serve."

God heard the Apostle Paul's fervent prayers for the deliverance of the ship and all those on board. God sent an angel that stood before the Apostle Paul and explained that God would deliver him from the storm to stand in front of Caesar in Rome.

The Apostle Paul was a great man of faith that God recognized and blessed. It was the Apostle Paul's fervent prayers that God answered and sent his angel to deliver His response. This angel was sent by God for a number of different reasons. God ensured Paul that his prayers were heard and that he was in God's plan. The angel also explained that the storm would end and that all would be saved. All 276 people on the ship would benefit from Paul's faith and leadership.

Paul never forgot to pray for the churches and their specific needs. In Colossians the Apostle Paul's prayer is focused on the needs within the church at Colossae.

Colossians 1: 9–12 reads, "For this cause we also, since the day we heard it, do not cease to pray for you, and to desire that ye might be filled with the knowledge of his will in all wisdom and spiritual understanding; That ye might walk worthy of the Lord unto all pleasing, being fruitful in every good work, and increasing in the knowledge of God; Strengthened with all might, according to his glorious power, unto all patience and long-suffering with joyfulness; Giving thanks unto the Father, which hath made us meet to be partakers of the inheritance of the saints in light:"

Paul's prayers included a request for a thorough understanding of God's will for all of mankind. This would include having the ability to accumulate spiritual principals found in scripture and applying them to our daily lives. Paul's daily prayers always included the needs of the church and all of the members. Specific needs for the church included strength to endure all of the challenges, patience to endure suffering, and restraint to avoid retaliation.

Our prayers need to be addressed to our God the Creator of the universe and the church. We worship God the Father and through Him alone we are dependent on Him for our salvation.

We may experience a number of shipwrecks as we travel through our lives. We need to be in prayer that God would hear our prayers and send His protection and peace when the time is right. Like Paul, we need to remember that there may be others that are dependent on us to maintain a close relationship with our Lord and Savior. We need to be a blessing to others.

John the Apostle

THE APOSTLE JOHN WAS transformed from a fisherman to a messenger of God. His life was devoted to making God known and the saving grace of His Son, Jesus Christ.

John 19: 25–27 reads, "Now there stood by the cross of Jesus his mother, and his mother's sister, Mary the wife of Cleophas, and Mary Magdalene. When Jesus therefore saw his mother, and the disciple standing by, whom he loved, he saith unto his mother, Woman behold thy son! Then saith he to the disciple, Behold thy mother! And from that hour that disciple took her unto his own home."

The very last words spoken by Jesus are directed at his beloved mother and disciples. Jesus' death on the cross paid for all of man's sin. From that time forward John and the disciples ensured that Jesus' mother (Mary) would be protected and that all of her needs would be met. The danger was great with the Sanhedrin and now the Roman Government was willing to execute those that are found guilty of blasphemy. Members of the Sanhedrin were looking for all those who were associated with Jesus. Consequently, John and the Apostles went to great lengths to ensure that Jesus' mother (Mary) was protected and out of danger.

John was called the beloved Apostle by Jesus and a messenger from God. He was the youngest of the Apostles and lived a long life, and was believed to have died in Ephesus at the age of ninety four. It is generally agreed that the Apostle John was responsible for writing the Gospel of John, three Epistles of John, and Book of Revelations. It is believed he moved from Israel between 33AD to 70AD with his family and extended family (including Mary the mother of Jesus) to support the Apostle Paul and the churches he started in Ephesus. The Apostle Paul died about 67 AD and the Apostle Peter died about 64 AD which left the Apostle John as the oldest original Apostle living from 64 AD to about 100 AD. This placed the Apostle John in the leadership role of the Ephesus church and subject to all the responsibilities. In about 95 AD he was banished to the Island of Patmos for a period of time and eventually returned to the church of Ephesus.

The Roman Government had increased its efforts to eliminate the Christian church by capturing its leaders and placing them in prison or charging them with some type of punishment such as banishment. The Apostle John was arrested and banished to the small island of Patmos. These small islands did have mines where criminals were forced to work under extreme conditions.

As a Son of Thunder, the Apostle John had experienced a great deal of joy and sorrow. While imprisoned on the Island of Patmos the Apostle John began to be given great insights by the Holy Spirit. He was able to record these ideas and visions that would be later become the book of Revelation. The Apostle John also had students such as Polycarp and others that studied under his direction.

It is believed that the Apostle John was eventually released from Patmos and returned to Ephesus as head of the Church of Ephesus. The Apostle John was the last of the Apostles and died in Ephesus at an age greater than 90.

John's life was an example to all of mankind, as to how to live a life under persecution and suffering. The Holy Spirit directed The Apostle John to write down his visions and to send it to seven churches. The Holy Spirit is working with Christians today and directing them to live a life that is focused on spreading the saving message of the gospel.

Learning to be a Servant

We are all unique individuals that have been exposed to many different and unique and in some cases similar experiences. How we learn and in some cases not learn from these experiences is in a great deal determined by abilities and environment.

John and his older brother the Apostle James (James the Greater) were also called by Jesus as the Sons of Thunder. Both men had little patience and when pushed to their limits would speak out loudly and chastise people for their sinful nature.

Luke 9:53–56 reads, "And they did not receive him, because his face was as though he would go to Jerusalem. And when his disciples James and John saw this, they said, Lord, wilt thou that we command fire to come down from heaven, and consume them, even as Elijah did? But he turned, and rebuked them, and said, Ye know not what manner of spirit ye are of. For the Son of man is not come to destroy man's lives, but to save them. And they went to another village."

However, both men were reprimanded by Jesus and they both seemed to be able keep their temper under control. The Apostle Johns' writings do at times reflect shortness with those that do not believe and are not willing to change their lives. John's writings reflected a long life that was filled with many experiences such as the crucifixion of his Lord and Savior, the death of other beloved Apostles, the death of his brother James, and the teachings of Jesus. The Apostle John's life was transformed, changing a young man with great intensity to an old man with great wisdom where faith became vision. These changes were made in spite of John's make-up. In other words Jesus is able to mold a man into what he chooses regardless of past experiences.

The Apostle John was a student that sat at the feet of his Master for three years, absorbing as much as humanly possible. He watched and experienced the washing of his feet by his Lord and Savior, Jesus. This simple act had a profound impact on John's understanding of what it meant to be a servant of the Lord. The fact that Jesus (God's only Son) would wash his feet, a task for a lowly servant, was difficult to understand, extremely humbling, and unbelievable. John was learning that we are servants to the gospel and that it is our mission in this life is to teach and preach the saving grace of God's word throughout the world. John grew to be a man of great passion, humility, and at the same time a man of great courage.

The Apostle John's life on the Island of Patmos was similar to that of Elijah. He lived in a cave where he was cut off from the outside world and was able to commune with his Lord and Savior. Both John and Elijah received prophetic revelations from God in this state where both men were being persecuted for preaching God's word. It was John being brandished to the Island of Patmos that allowed John to write the Book of Revelation.

Revelation 1:9 reads, "I John, who also am your brother, and companion in tribulation, and in the kingdom and patience of Jesus Christ, was in the isle that is called Patmos, for the word of god, and for the testimony of Jesus Christ."

The instruction John received from Jesus allowed him to serve his time on Patmos with an attitude of servitude, patience, and endurance knowing that his earthly experience would be met with grace and the glory of his heavenly Father.

The Apostle John was called the Beloved Apostle by Jesus. The Apostle John was passionate about the true word of God and how it affected all of God's creation. He was concerned about man's relationship with his Heavenly Father and the need to love your neighbor, to be obedient God's word, and to be forgiving.

A servant to God is being loyal and obedient even when it is not popular. Society's attitude toward Christians has drifted from persecution to indifference. We should be focused on achieving and maintaining a reputation as being honest, righteous, and just. We need to humble ourselves and live a life of integrity.

The Apostle John and Family

The Apostle John was taught by Jesus, traveled and ate with Jesus, and was present when Jesus healed the sick, raised the dead, and cast out demons. He was witness to thousands being converted from a life of sin and death to a life full of eternal grace. These experiences changed the Apostle John in many ways. He became a person with a positive attitude, his focus was on others, and he was passionate about sharing God's truth with all of mankind regardless of the risks.

Ephesians 4:15 reads, "But speaking the truth in love, may grow up into him in all things, which is the head even Christ."

The Apostle John grew to be a man that spoke the word of God in love. God's words are spoken with the purpose of turning a life away from sin to a life of Grace. God's words are spoken in confidence, with grace, humility, and compassion. There is no room for pride, boasting, or self. When we see and hear the braggart, the boaster, the know it all, it is difficult to see anything beyond that lack of respect. We are to encourage one another to develop their gifts so that the church may grow and all may share in those gifts. The church is a living functioning body that is dependent on each member to engage and contribute their gifts.

The Apostle John was also aware of rejection by family and friends. The Apostles traveled with Jesus to Nazareth where he spent his childhood and spoke in the synagogue. Jesus read from Isaiah and explained that he was the Messiah.

Isaiah 61:1 reads, "The spirit of the Lord God is upon me; because the Lord hath anointed me to preach good tidings unto the meek; he hath sent me to bind up the broken hearted, to proclaim liberty to the captives, and the opening of the prison to them that are bound."

The family and friends of Jesus could only see that Jesus was the son of a carpenter and nothing more. They became offended by what Jesus was saying and forced him to leave the synagogue and Nazareth. Family dynamics are complex and involve a history of attitudes, opinions, and experiences. It is not uncommon for family members to resist or acknowledge success or changes made by another member. Some of these difficulties are psychosomatic and some are simply a refusal to acknowledge that sin exists and they need to consider allowing Jesus to resolve their many problems. The Apostle John was able to gain a deeper understanding from Jesus of the pain and anguish that one experiences when family and friends do not accept the gospel and the saving grace of the Lord Jesus.

The Apostle John was the head of the church of Ephesus for about thirty years. During this time The Roman Empire ruled the Mediterranean area with an iron fist. Any type of revolt or unrest was met with severe punishment by either death or imprisonment that resulted in thousands of Jews being slaughtered or being enslaved and sent to Rome. The Christians during this time were considered a cult that was responsible for unrest and conflicts with the Jews. Many of the people were highly superstitious and worshiped pagan gods and blamed the Christians for any hardship. In 64 AD the Christians were blamed for the great fire in Rome and as a result many were burned or put to death. In spite of all the persecution, the church grew during this thirty year period of time that the Apostle John was head of the church. It has been estimated that 28% of the people in the area had heard God's word and it was preached in 6 different languages.

Family life can be complicated and maybe difficult. Today, even the weather has become more unpredictable and severe. Disease has become a greater concern for families as they struggle to maintain a consistent inflow of income to meet family related costs at an ever increasing inflation rate.

Deuteronomy 31:8 reads, "And the Lord, he it is that doth go before thee; he will be with thee, he will not fail thee, neither forsake thee: fear not, neither be dismayed."

The Apostle John's Love for the Church

IT WAS THE APOSTLE John's ministry to encourage the Gentile Christians to realize the importance of their heavenly origin and their future with their Creator, but also to realize the responsibility to live a life on earth as those chosen of God and sealed by the Holy Spirit.

The Apostle John was a man of truth and taught the truth from the beginning for the purpose that all could have fellowship with The Holy Spirit, The Son and with The Father.

It was John's ministry that focused on the building up of the Gentiles and teaching them the law. The Apostle John's love for the church of Ephesus was repeated throughout his writings.

Revelations 2:1–3 reads, "Unto the angels of the church of Ephesus write; These things saith he that holdeth the seven stars in his right hand, who walketh in the midst of the seven golden candlesticks; I know thy works, and thy labor, and thy patience, and how thou canst not bear them which are evil: and thou hast tried them which say they are apostles, and are not, and hast found them liars. And hast borne, and hast patience, and for my names sake hast labored, and hast not fainted."

The Apostle John was persistently faithful throughout his entire life. It was Peter and John that ran together to the sepulcher the morning of the resurrection. The Apostle John experienced a great deal in his life. John changed because he had three years of training with his Savior and Lord; experienced the death and resurrection of his Savior and Lord, and saw Him later in His risen body. He experienced the death of his brother James and the death and beating of many more Apostles and early Christians. John's temperament grew to be one of great love and understanding. He was thoughtful and was able to sense God's will in each situation. John was a trusted Apostle that could be counted on and would be loved by all. It was John's love for the Church of Ephesus that caused his concern for all the members.

1 John 5:21 reads, "Little children keep yourselves from idols. Amen."

The pagan life in Ephesus was permeated with idols in virtually every aspect of daily life. It was only through the power of the Holy Spirit that these first converts to Christianity were able to separate themselves from pagan life and learn how to love others and obey God's commandments. It is only at that point when a true understanding of God's will is realized that a fervent love for others and a love for obedience began to grow.

The Apostle John and his life's work was always centered on the truth and the fruit of the Holy Spirit and love.

John 3:16 reads, "For God so loved the world, that he gave his only begotten Son, that whosoever believeth in him should not perish, but have everlasting life."

John 14:15 reads, "If ye love me, keep my commandments."

1 John 3:10–11 reads, "In this the children of God are manifest, and the children of the devil: whosoever doeth not righteousness is not of God, nether he that loveth not his brother. For this is the message that ye heard from the beginning, that we should love one another."

1 John 4:7–12 reads, "Beloved, let us love one another: for love is of God; and everyone that loveth is born of God, and knoweth God. He that loveth not knoweth not God; for God is love. In this was manifested the love of God toward us, because that God sent his only begotten Son into the world, that we might live through him. Herein is love, not that we loved God, but that he loved us, and sent his Son to be the propitiation for our sin. Beloved, if God so loved us, we ought also to love one another. No man hath seen God at any time. If we love one another, God dwelleth in us, and his love is perfected in us."

Loving Your Neighbor

1 John 5:2–3 reads, "By this we know that we love the children of God, when we love God, and keep his commandments. For this is the love of God, that we keep his commandments: and his commandments are not grievous."

More than any other disciple the Apostle John spoke and wrote about loving your neighbor and following the commandments.

Matthew 22: 37–40 reads, "Jesus said unto him, Thou shalt love Lord thy God with all thy heart, and with all thy soul, and with all thy mind. This is the first and great commandment. And the second is like unto it, thou shalt love thy neighbor as thyself. On these two commandments hang all the law and the prophets."

The Apostle John was following Jesus' teachings that loving the Lord God with all your heart, soul and mind is paramount for a person to begin a personal relationship with their Creator. This is a natural desire that God has placed within each person that cannot be filled by any accomplishment, possession, and any amount of wealth. The Holy Spirit will change each person that is willing to open their heart, soul, and mind and will convict them of the need to obey God's commandments.

The Apostle John spent his entire adult life teaching about God's love for His creation. The people of Ephesus were lost in a culture that worshiped stone idols in the hope that they would receive a better life. They had hundreds of priests that were well versed in mythology and would tell them about the many pagan gods and goddesses. However, there was no one that knew about Jesus Christ and the saving grace that was available to all of mankind. There was no one that knew that the Creator of all mankind sacrificed His Only Son so that all of mankind may be allowed access to life everlasting. There was no one that knew that the greatest commandment was to love God with all your heart, with your soul, and with all your mind. And, to love your neighbor as you would love yourself. Obviously, the Apostle John and the Church of Ephesus had the tremendous challenge to preach the message of the gospel under the continual threat of persecution and possible death.

The Ephesus church and the other churches in the area were struggling with people that knew only of the pagan gods that they had always worshiped. They were worshiping these pagan gods hoping their needs for food, shelter, pleasure, greed, wealth, envy, and others would be met. There were pagan gods for every need including acts of perversion, satanic, and debauchery. There were few or no moral standards and the people were only subject to Roman Laws and the opinions of priests at the Ephesusʼ temples.

A pagan god is anything that prevents you from worshiping our Lord and Savior. Anything that takes priority or prevents you from worshiping our Lord and Savior is a pagan god. The people of today as the people of Ephesus are focused on self and experiencing as much pleasure as possible. The church is no longer a priority.

In Europe today you see many grand magnificent churches that are no longer used as churches. They are in many cases being maintained and managed by different governments. In some cases they are being destroyed or being used for other purposes rather than for worship. These churches were built by thousands of saints that sacrificed a great deal of time and money so that many generations may have a place to worship their Creator.

The Apostle John was able to write the Book of Revelation with divine intervention from God. At the age of ninety two John was imprisoned on the Island of Patmos. This remote island in the Aegean Sea was used by the Romans as a prison for political and religious prisoners and for mining. Johnʼs crime was his continual preaching of Jesusʼ saving Grace to those in Ephesus.

Revelation 1:1 reads, "The Revelation of Jesus Christ, which God gave unto him, to show unto his servants things which must shortly come to pass; and he sent and signified it by his angel unto his servant John."

Sin in the World

THERE IS ONE BIBLE and that Bible contains the Old Testament and New Testament. There are many definitions and explanations as to what sin is within the Bible and how to avoid it and how to withstand it's temptations. We also know God hates sin, but loves the sinner. Today, many businesses and people are trying to convince people that sin no longer exists.

There are many verses in the Bible that explains how sin will destroy the relationship between God and man. The Bible states many times that if you love God you will keep His commandments.

1 John 5:2–4 reads, "By this we know that we love the children of God, when we love God, and keep his commandments. For this is the love of God, that we keep his commandments: and his commandments are not grievous. For whosoever is born of God overcometh the world: and this is the victory that overcometh the world, even our faith."

Matthew 5:17 reads, "Think not that I am come to destroy the law, or the prophets: I am not come to destroy, but to fulfill."

The New Testament is the fulfillment of the spiritual intent of the Old Testament. The birth of Jesus, His teachings, His crucifixion, and resurrection were all prophesized in the Old Testament.

The first commandment states we should love God with all our hearts, mind, and soul and not to have any others gods. God should be the most important thing in our lives.

Matthew 22:37–39 reads, "Jesus said unto him, Thou Shalt Love The Lord Thy God With All Thy Heart, And With All Thy Soul, And With All Thy Mind. This is the first and great commandment. And the second is like unto it, Thou Shalt Love Thy Neighbor As Thyself."

We all live in a fallen state and are born in a world that is filled with sin. The sin we encounter on a daily basis is to surrender to the world's values. The world's focus is to worship money rather than worship God.

We need to guard our language and not use God's name in vain. Each individual should keep holy the Sabbath day. Not to honor our father and mother is a sin and to steal from others is a sin. To murder an innocent person is a sin. Adultery is a sin for a man and woman who are married. To lie or to deceive another person is a sin. To lust after a women or a man is a sin. Human sexuality is a divine gift and is only appropriate between a married man and woman. The feelings of envy, greed, and jealousy are all sins and should be rejected.

1 John 2:16 reads, "For all that is in world, the lust of the flesh, and the lust of the eyes, and the pride of life, is not of the Father, but is of world."

The Apostle Paul loved the new churches in Galatia and wanted to protect them from the pagans and the great liar. He told them that the sins of the pagan would bring them death.

Galatians 5:19–21 reads, "Now the works of the flesh are manifest, which are these; adultery, fornication, uncleanness, lasciviousness, Idolatry, witchcraft, hatred, variance, emulations, wrath, strife, seditions, heresies, envying, murders, drunkenness, revellings, and such like: of the which I tell you before, as I have also told you in time past, that they which do such things shall not inherit the kingdom of God."

1 John 1:9 reads, "If we confess our sins, he is faithful and just to forgive us our sins, and to cleanse us from all unrighteousness."

God has provided an escape from these sins with the gift of His only Son, Jesus the Savior.

Salvation for All

GOD IS THE CREATOR of all things in the heavens and on the earth. God formed man from the dust of the ground and breathed into him the breath of life so that he may become a living soul. God also created woman from one of Adam's ribs. The creation of woman made man complete.

God allowed Adam the freedom to eat from any tree except for one, the tree of knowledge of good and evil. Satan is the great liar and he convinced Eve she would become a god if she disobeyed God.

Genesis 2:17 reads, "But of the tree of the knowledge of good and evil, thou shalt not eat of it: for in the day that thou eatest thereof thou shalt surely die."

The eating of the fruit from the tree of knowledge of good and evil resulted in the spiritual death of Adam and Eve. This disobedience by Adam and Eve resulted in the separation for all of mankind from God.

However, God did provide for a way for salvation. Abraham was able to bridge this separation with his faith in God. Abraham lived 400 years before the law.

Genesis 15:6 reads, "And he believed in the Lord; and he counted it to him for righteousness."

Romans 4:3 reads, "For what saith the scripture? Abraham believed God, and it was counted unto him for righteousness."

The Bible is clear in both the Old Testament and New Testament that the way to salvation is by faith.

Ephesians 2:8–9 reads, "For by grace are ye saved through faith, and that not of yourselves: it is the gift of God: Not off works, lest any man should boast:"

When Adam and Eve sinned they were driven from the Garden and the presence of God. The wages of sin is spiritual death. The only way for

God to reunite with man was through the ultimate sacrifice of God's only Son, Jesus Christ. There is a price related to our sin.

God loves us regardless of our many sins. He is patiently waiting for us to confess our sins and to ask for Him to come into our lives and to take control of our lives. At that time the Holy Spirit will commune with our souls and to begin to convict us of our many sins. The greatest gift we will ever receive in this life is the sacrifice of Jesus' life on the cross.

Zephaniah 3:17 reads, "The Lord thy God in the midst of thee is mighty; he will save, he will rejoice over thee with joy; he will rest in his love, he will joy over thee with singing."

Luke 15:32 reads, "It was meet that we should make merry, and be glad: for this thy brother was dead, and is alive again; and was lost, and is found."

There is great joy and celebration in heaven for each sinner who repents.

The Apostle Paul and the Apostle Peter

THE APOSTLE PAUL AND the Apostle Peter were very different people with different personalities and different backgrounds. But, God used these two different people to further the gospel in a mighty way.

The Apostle Peter was one of the first Apostles Jesus selected to join the group of twelve Apostles. Peter a fisherman was initially a disciple of John the Baptist and started following Jesus after the baptism of Jesus. Peter was an impetuous man that would actually challenge Jesus if he did not understand God's purpose or plan. Peter's love for Jesus was without question and he was ready to use his use his sword to defend Jesus if needed.

As a Jew and raised in a Jewish home, Peter would have been required to study Jewish law and customs.

It is estimated that The Apostle Paul (Saul of Tarsus) was born around 5 BC to 5 AD, a number of years after the crucifixion and the resurrection of Jesus the Messiah. Saul was a Pharisee that took pride in the persecution of the early followers of Jesus. Saul was struck blind for three days and his sight was restored by Ananias of Damascus.

Acts 9:3–5 reads, "And as he journeyed, he came near Damascus: and suddenly there shines round about him a light from heaven: And he fell to the earth, and heard a voice saying unto him, Saul, Saul, why persecutes thou me?"

God spoke directly to Saul asking him why he was persecuting His followers. Saul response was, "what should I do."

God also spoke directly to Ananias and told him to go to Saul. Ananias was fearful knowing Saul's reputation as a person who persecuted many Christians.

Acts 9:15–16 reads, "But the lord said unto him, Go thy way: for he is a chosen vessel unto me, to bear my name before the Gentiles, and kings, and the children of Israel. For I will show him how great things he must suffer for my name's sake."

Nothing is impossible for God. He can take the Saul's of this world and turn them into great men of faith. We must continue to pray and not underestimate God's power to bring about change when all other avenues have been closed. What may seem impossible and not reasonable may be possible and part of God's plan.

God is always loving and patient with those He loves. The Apostle Peter was continually making mistakes, but God was exceedingly patient with Peter. God asked Peter if he loved him three times.

John 21:17 reads, "He saith unto him the third time, Simon, son of Jonah, lovest thou me? Peter was grieved because he said unto him the third time, Lovest thou me? And he said unto him, Lord, thou knowest all things; thou knowest that I love thee. Jesus saith unto him, Feed my sheep.

If you love God you must feed his sheep. Feeding God's people may involve sharing the gospel in many different ways. Peter shared the gospel with both the Gentiles and the Jews.

The Apostle John's Life on Patmos

It is generally believed that The Apostle John was exiled to the Greek island of Patmos by Roman authorities because of his Christian teachings. The Apostle John and the Christian community were considered to be a political threat by the Roman government.

God's messenger an angel was sent to John for the purpose of sharing God's word in the Book of Revelation. The book reveals God plan for mankind centered around God's only Son, Jesus Christ.

John's relationship with God's angel of interpretation was over a period of time to complete the Book of Revelation. At one point John begins to worship this angel and is quickly told to stop by the angel.

Revelation 19:10 reads, "And I fell at his feet to worship him. And he said unto me, See thou do it not: I am thy fellow servant, and of thy brethren that have the testimony of Jesus: worship God: for the testimony of Jesus is the spirit of prophecy."

We are commanded to only worship God. All of all our possessions, experiences, achievements and our very breath were given to us by God and belong to Him.

Many of the younger generation of today have fallen prey to the same temptations that all men have fallen to since the beginning of time. They are focused on self and the worship of wealth, pleasure, status and anything that will satisfy their greed. These are the same issues that Moses, Elijah, Peter, James, and John had to deal with. Pagan gods have always been a temptation for man since they appeal to man's greed and sense of self.

The basic mission of the Apostle John as well as other saints was to minister to all of man that their Creator loved them and had provided a way for their salvation through his Son, Jesus the Christ. In addition, God was patiently waiting for them to realize that they needed to worship the all powerful, all knowing God and ever present God; their Creator.

The Apostle John was a loving and compassionate man that spent his life serving God's people and ministering the message of salvation to the world. It is believed that during his last years he was carried to church so that he may worship with the people of the church of Ephesus. It is believed that his last words were; children love one another.

The Apostle John was called "John the Evangelist" and "John the beloved disciple". He was present at the crucifixion and death of Jesus. In fact, Jesus called out to John while hanging of the cross.

John 19:26–27 reads, "When Jesus therefore saw his mother, and the disciple standing by whom he loved, he saith unto his mother, Women behold thy son! Then saith he to the disciple, Behold they mother! And from that hour that disciple took her unto his own home."

Jesus (God's only Son) while breathing his last breath on the cross honored His mother and the beloved disciple, John. From that time forward the Apostle John would be consigned to care for Mary, the mother of Jesus.

The Holy Spirit

We worship a Triune God who has existed for eternity. The Triune God consists of God the Father, God the Son, and God the Holy Spirit. God the Father is the creator of all things and designs the plans for all of man and all things. God the Son is fully man and fully God and is completely obedient to God the Father. God the Holy Spirit indwells man's soul.

Man invites the Holy Spirit into his life with a prayer. The prayer begins by acknowledging the fact that we are all sinners and asking for forgiveness for those many sins. We invite God to enter into our lives and turn away from all sin. We ask God to become our Lord and Savior and to direct our lives.

1 John 1:9 reads, "If we confess our sins, he is faithful and just for forgive us our sins, and to cleanse us from all unrighteousness."

Romans 10:9 reads, "That if thou shalt confess with thy mouth the Lord Jesus, and shalt believe in thine heart that God hath raised him from the dead, thou shalt be saved."

Salvation and the grace of God are delivered to man by his faith.

Ephesians 2:8–9 reads, "For by grace are ye saved through faith; and that not of yourselves: it is the gift of God: Not of works, lest any man should boast."

Many people confess to be Christians, but their lives do not reflect the values and morals of a Christian.

Man's spirit lives at the center of his soul and allows man to commune with God's Holy Spirit. Once a person makes the decision to accept Jesus into their life, God's Holy Spirit enters man's spiritual body and begins to provide man with His many gifts. These gifts include wisdom, conviction of sin, recognition of righteousness, fear of God, increased faith, patience, and discernment.

The initial impact of the confession of sins and the admission of a sin filled life can be dramatic. The Holy Spirit will convict a person of their sin and force them to face the fact that they need to make a change in their life. They come to the realization that they cannot continue to live in sin if they want to grow closer to God.

1 Peter 5:8 reads, "Be sober, be vigilant: because your adversary the devil, as a roaring lion, walketh about, seeking whom he may devour:"

1 Timothy 6:11–12 reads, "But thou, O man of God, flee these things; and follow after righteousness, godliness, faith, love, patience, meekness. Fight the good fight of faith, lay hold on eternal life, whereunto thou art also called, and hast professed a good profession before many witnesses."

We need to be careful not to be ensnared by the devil as he skillfully plans ways to entrap Christians in sin. Satan is keenly aware of man's weaknesses and will use those weaknesses (e.g. pride of life) to convince man there is nothing wrong with sin.

Yes, Jesus did engage sinners and spoke to them about their sin. He loves the sinner, but hates the sin. In fact, Jesus commanded the disciples and Christians to go out throughout the world and preach the gospel. Jesus made salvation available to all of mankind and at any time. Jesus allowed the thief on the cross to enter heaven after he made a decision to believe that Jesus was the Savior of the world.

Luke 23:43 reads, "And Jesus said unto him, Verily I say unto thee, Today shalt thou be with me in paradise."

Jesus allowed this thief to enter paradise minutes before he died. There does not seem to be any time limit as to when a decision may be made to accept the free gift of salvation.

Evil People

Evil people have always existed since the creation of mankind. God gave man free will and allowed him to decide whether to follow the path to righteousness or to evil. A detailed study of evil people and why they immerse themselves in evil practices is beyond the scope of this book and has filled many bookshelves in libraries.

People without a conscious are the most dangerous, unpredictable, and difficult to understand. Throughout history the world has seen people that commit unspeakable crimes against humanity that are incomprehensible to the average person. Some of these evil behaviors were the result of a reaction to traumatic childhood experiences.

Many of these evil people are highly skilled at hiding their evil traits and manipulating their victims. A first time meeting with these individuals will probably not detect any abnormal character traits.

Our society is fixated on materialism and readily accepts and promotes any idea that is focused on greed, consumption, and wealth. Consequently, narcissistic people who view all of life as to how it effects them, will have an inflated ego and spend much of their life trying to impress others with their accomplishments.

Society today expects its citizens to accept and embrace any and all behavior, even the behavior that is contrary to God's word. Some Christians believe all people should be loved regardless of the evil they are practicing.

Romans 12:9 reads, "Let love be without dissimulation. Abhor that which is evil; cleave to that which is good."

The Holy Spirit provides guidance as to how to love your neighbor and at the same time abhor the evil that they may be practicing.

Ephesians 5:11 reads, "And have no fellowship with the unfruitful works of darkness, but rather reprove them."

The Christian should not have any relationship with the works of evil. The Christian should not be involved in promoting evil or indulge in evil practices. If anything, the Christian should be exposing evil whenever possible. There is a real danger in developing a relationship with a narcissist, sociopath, or psychopath individual. Many of these people will kill with no empathy for their victims and will justify their actions as a means to achieving a greater goal.

God washed the earth clean of sin and evil with the flood. God erased sin and evil when He destroyed the cities of Sodom and Gomorrah with fire. God eliminated an entire generation of Israelites due to sin and evil. God gave His Son as a sacrifice for the forgiveness of sins and evil for the entire world.

The importance of recognizing and eliminating sin and evil in the world cannot be minimized. Satan is extremely cunning and able to confuse the most intelligent people of this world.

1 Peter 5:8 reads, "Be Sober, be vigilant; because your adversary the devil, as a roaring lion, walketh about, seeking whom he may devour:"

Believers in God will be Persecuted

Believers in The One True God have been persecuted since the beginning of time. The degree of suffering has varied from being a slave under the rule of the Pharaoh's in Egypt to being imprisoned today in China. The battle between good and evil has always existed but The One True God is a loving, kind, and forgiving God.

Some Christians may be surprised when they go through a time of trials and suffering. We should not fear for God will strengthen us and help us in the time of need.

1 Peter 1:7 reads, "That the trial of your faith, being much more precious than of gold that perisheth, through it be tried with fire, might be found unto praise and honor and glory at the appearing of Jesus Christ:"

Our faith in God is priceless and will open the doors to eternity for the believer. Our faith brings honor, praise, and glory to Jesus our Lord and Savior.

James 1:12 reads, "Blessed is the man that endureth temptation: for when he is tried, he shall receive the crown of life, which the Lord hath promised to them that loved him."

Suffering and trials may at first seem to appear as a curse, but they may be used by God as an avenue for delivering blessings. Endurance and strength can be built as a believer masters different situations and is able to manage different personalities and situations.

God is faithful and only allows temptations into our lives that we are able to handle.

1 Corinthian 10:13 reads, "There hath no temptation taken you but such as is common to man: but God is faithful, who will not suffer you to be tempted above that ye are able; but will with the temptation also make a way to escape, that ye may be able to bear it."

A believer may have difficult situations that enter their lives on a daily basis. They have the opportunity to strengthen their relationship with God if they obey God's directions. They also have the opportunity to promote evil, doubt God's direction, and disobey God.

God may allow temptations to enter a person's life that he can endure and if necessary He will also provide a way of escape.

Narrow is the Way

The way to salvation is available to all of mankind. However, there are many who fall to the many temptations that sin and the world offers.

Matthew 7:13–14 reads, "Enter ye in at the strait gate: for wide is the gate, and broad is the way, that leadeth to destruction, and many there be which go in thereat. Because strait is the gate, and narrow is the way, which leadeth unto life, and few there be that find it."

The gate is wide and open to all. However, few are able to follow the path to salvation due to the many temptations leading to destruction. Many reject the gift of salvation and choose to believe in their own philosophies, abilities and pride.

Jesus corrected the Apostle John and the Apostle James and told them that he would not destroy a village because he came to save lives and not to destroy them. Jesus again showed his love and patience for the Samaritans and allowed them more time to make a decision of commitment to Christianity.

We need to be careful not to rush to judgment of others. God has a plan for each and every man and only He will make the final judgment. However, we should run from evil and not entertain evil practices and ideas.

Proverbs 3: 5–7 reads, "Trust in the Lord with all thine heart; and lean not unto thine own understanding. In all thine ways acknowledge him, and he shall direct thy paths. Be not wise in thine own eyes: fear the Lord, and depart from evil."

As Christians we live a life that is protected by God and His angels. We can take comfort in knowing no matter how difficult the situation God is always in control and He is our protector from all evil. God at any time can send down His angels to guard us from any evil that we may encounter.

Angels are spoken of throughout the Bible in many different situations and for many different purposes.

Psalm 91:11 reads, "For he shall give his angels charge over thee, to keep thee in all thy ways."

Satan is aggressively attacking today's youth with many of the world's temptations. Many youth are being exposed to drugs, alcohol, and criminal activity at a younger age each year. In many cases there is no supervision or monitoring of children when they are not in the classroom. Some parents have little or no involvement with children's after school activity. Children with little contact with parents will find a sense of family with gangs. These gangs can provide a child with a sense of family, money and self worth. A gang may require a child to steal a car in order for that child to be accepted as a member of the gang.

Being accepted and loved by a family is a powerful emotion that most youth would desire and take a risk to achieve. In some cases the desire to be a member of a gang is so great that a child will kill another person to meet that membership requirement.

Like children, adults live out their lives wanting to be wanted. In some cases, adults will go to extremes to get the acceptance and attention of a group, community, or state. The desire to be accepted in some cases may take priority over other relationships. For example, a mother may neglect the safety of a child in order to meet with a friend. Parenting patterns and value systems are passed on from generation to generation. Consequently, to break or change these cycles of bad behavior would require direct and frequent counseling.

2 Corinthians 5:17 reads, "Therefore if any man be in Christ, he is a new creature: old things are passed away; behold, all things are become new."

Loving Your Neighbor

Jesus was asked by the lawyers what is the most important command-ment? He responded by saying man needs to love God with all his heart and to love His neighbor as he loves himself.

Matthew 22:37–39 reads, "Jesus said unto him, Thou shalt love the Lord thy God with all thy heart, and with all thy soul, and with all thy mind. This is the first and great commandment. And the second is like unto it, thou shalt love thy neighbor as thyself."

How a person loves themselves does vary dramatically. They gener-ally try to meet the basic need for clothing, the procurement of food with a living wage, and secure shelter that is comfortable. Therefore, meeting the basic needs of our neighbor would include enough food for the family, clothing for all the seasons, and comfortable shelter. Other needs may in-clude the washing of clothes, training costs related to meeting requirements for employment, and possibly consulting.

However, there are those that love themselves excessively by taking endless photos of themselves, spending many hours in front of a mirror, spending millions of dollars on skin products, etc. Still others spend mil-lions on vacations, spend millions on entertainment, and spend millions on other luxury purchases. Many of these same individuals are also extremely greedy and selfish and spend little or nothing on those in need.

Our neighbor is anyone who is in need.

A good Samaritan stopped and cared for a man that was attacked by thieves and left on the side of a road for dead. The thieves are still with us today and they are still completing unspeakable acts of violence against their neighbors.

Luke 10:34–35 reads, "And went to him, and bound up his wounds, pouring in oil and wine, and set him on his own beast, and brought him in an inn, and took care of him. And on the morrow when he departed, he took out two pence, and gave them to the host, and said unto him, Take care of him; and whatsoever thou spendest more, when I come again, I will repay thee."

Showing love for your neighbor in need can be taken on in many different ways.

Man was created in God's image and was designed for the purpose of worshiping, maintaining and building God's creations. Man's soul and spirit are able to grow with the care and nurturing of the Holy Spirit. It is only when this relationship is established that true joy and peace are realized.

Psalm 1:1–2 reads, "Blessed is the man that walketh not in the counsel of the ungodly, nor standeth in the way of sinners, nor sitteth in the seat of the scornful. But his delight is in the law of the Lord; and in his law doth he mediate day and night."

Following God's law and showing love to your neighbor needs to be applied together in prayer. We need to be sensitive to the relationship between our soul and spirit and God's Holy Spirit. We should begin each day in prayer thanking God for the gift of eternal life, thanking God for His many blessings, and asking God for forgiveness for the many sins we continue to commit.

1 John 1:9 reads, "If we confess our sins, he is faithful and just to forgive us our sins, and to cleanse us from all unrighteousness."

Maintaining a Christ-like life requires an ongoing process of identifying sin as it appears in its many forms in our daily lives and asking for forgiveness.

You Know Not What Ye Ask

The Apostle James had a burning evangelical zeal for the gospel. He preached to many in Israel and possibly Spain. His preaching was fearless, loud, forceful, effective, and he soon developed a reputation with the Jewish Synagogues. He was challenging the Jewish leadership, their laws and beliefs and caused them to conspire with the Romans to have him silenced.

It is believed it was James' fiery preaching that helped to ignite the spread of the gospel throughout Israel and possibly in Spain. The Apostle James was a threat to the Jewish leadership and a problem for the Roman leadership. The Apostle James continually repeated that Jesus was the true Messiah and the Savior of the world. It was James and John who said yes to Jesus when he asked can you drink from the cup.

Mark 10:38 reads, "But Jesus said unto them, Ye know not what ye ask: can ye drink of the cup that I drink of? And be baptized with the baptism that I am baptized with?"

The Apostle James knew what drinking the cup meant and He wanted to give his life for the sake of the gospel. He lived his life for one purpose and that one purpose was to preach the saving grace of the Lord Jesus Christ. As the Apostle James walked to his death, he was preaching the gospel of Christ and spoke of his joy to serve His Savior and Lord, the Messiah.

It had been about ten years since the Crucifixion of Jesus, and the death of the Apostle James would have had a traumatic impact on the Apostles. The death would have brought back the severe anguish and confusion when Jesus hung on the cross. They were reminded that their lives were in danger and especially now that King Herod realized that James' death curried favor from the Jews.

Today we need to renounce our many selfish desires and eliminate any selfish pursuit that is preventing a closer relationship with our Lord and Creator. We are followers of Jesus and are following His example that was devoted to helping others that are in need and to share the gospel of grace to those that have ears to hear. There are people waiting to hear you speak and to share your testimony so they too may rejoice as the Apostle James. As the Apostle James, we need to be willing to drink the cup, which means to share His suffering and death and love, and to give ourselves in the service of others. We are able to drink the cup because Jesus went before us and showed us the way that we too will experience the joy, the blessings, and life everlasting.

The Apostle James as the older brother of the Apostle John was a man of God and the first Apostle to be martyred. Jesus loved the Apostle James for his zeal, his fearlessness, his courage, and his impact on the conversion of the Jews and the Gentiles.

We know little about our life in heaven with Jesus our Lord and Savior. We know Jesus appeared to the disciples after His death on the cross. He allowed Thomas to touch his wounds from being huge on the cross.

John 20:27–29 reads, "Then saith he to Thomas, Reach hither thy finger, and behold my hands; and reach hither thy hands and thrust it into my side: and be not faithless, but believing. And Thomas answered and said unto him, My Lord and my God. Jesus saith unto him, Thomas, because thou hast seen me, thou hast believed: blessed are they that have not seen, and yet have believed."

The mother of James and John asked a question of Jesus hoping to get a favored position for her sons in heaven. There is a great deal about heaven and our standing as believers that we do not understand. However, God promised He has a place for us in heaven.

John 14:3 reads, "And if I go and prepare a place for you, I will come again, and receive you unto myself; that where I am, there ye may be also ."

Our Daily Focus

We are all focused upon our daily lives and the tasks that need to be completed. Many have grown to be extremely independent and rely on no one for support when confronted by difficulties. Some take no responsibility for their actions and will go to great lengths to blame others for their bad decisions. Many have developed strong defensive personality traits that are deployed when encountering difficult situations. The Christian has come to the realization that God is in control and that our first reaction to a difficult situation is prayer. A Christian shares many of life's difficulties and challenges with God in daily prayer and patiently waits for God's answer. The answer to difficult problems may come in many different ways and from many different sources. In some cases the answer is clear and in others cases the answer may be difficult to understand. Christians continually encourage each other to pray and ask God for all of their needs and desires.

Luke 11:9–10 reads, "And I say unto you, Ask, and it shall be given you; seek, and ye shall find; knock, and it shall be open unto you."

God's answer to prayers will be dependent on many different situations. First, God will not answer a Christian's prayer that will result in bringing harm to the Christian or those in his family. Just as parents are not willing to give their children harmful gifts, God will not give harmful gifts to Christians. Prayers are often made without a complete understanding of all those that may be effected by the request. Secondly, God knows the heart of each Christian and knows the motives behind each prayer and will respond accordingly. Another issue that may affect the answering of a prayer request may be the degree of obedience to God's commandments and statutes. There are many people that live each day in sin and refuse to admit they are living in sin.

Jesus was asked the question which commandment was the most important. Jesus' answer was to love God with all your heart, soul, and mind.

He also said to love your neighbor as yourself, and to obey all of God's commandments and statutes.

Matthew 22:35–40 reads, "Then one of them, which was a lawyer, asked him a question, temping him, and saying, Master, which is the great commandment in the law? Jesus said unto him, thou shalt love the Lord God with all thy heart, and with all thy soul, and with all thy mind. This is the first and great commandment. And the second is like unto it, thou shalt love thy neighbor as thyself. On these two commandments hang all the law and the prophets."

There is obviously a direct relationship between the loving of Almighty God and obeying His commandments. A Christian obeys God's commandments out of joy and not as an obedient slave. A Christian looks for opportunities to be obedient and enjoys the blessings of God's grace and peace. Today, man with Satan's support has twisted this simple principal into the idea that God created a fallen man that cannot obey God's commandments. God loves His creation and all of mankind. God gave His all, His only Son, that all who believe in Him will have eternal life. God not only gave His only Son he also gave us His word for study and direction.

The consequence for not accepting God's love and not obeying His commandments are incomprehensible.

Proverbs 28:9 reads, "He that turneth away his ear from hearing the law, even his prayer shall be abomination."

A Christian who breaks God's law will hinder the Holy Spirit that lives within him. The Holy Spirit requires a healthy mind and soul in order to convey and interpret our prayers to God.

The resurrection and the defeat of death by Jesus was a momentous event that was greeted with great joy in heaven. In this single event Jesus made it possible for all believers to spend eternity in heaven.

Birth of Jesus

God's angels were the messengers that delivered the joyous news of the birth of Jesus. The appearance of the first angel was a terrifying experience for the shepherds.

Luke 2:8–14 reads, "And there were in the same country shepherds abiding in the field, keeping watch over their flock by night. And, Lo, the angel of the Lord came upon them, and the glory of the Lord shone round about them: and they were sore afraid. And the angel said unto them, Fear not: for, behold, I bring you good tiding of great joy, which shall be to all people. For unto you is born this day in the city of David a Savior, which is Christ the Lord. And this shall be a sign unto you: Ye shall find the babe wrapped in swaddling clothes, lying in a manger. And suddenly there was with the angel a multitude of the heavenly host praising God, and saying, Glory to God in the highest, and on earth peace, good will toward men."

A great celebration took place as an army of angels raised their voices in joy over the birth of God's Son. The sky was filled with countless numbers of angels singing praises to God. This must have been an overwhelming experience for the shepherds. After the shepherds regained their composure they told others of what they had seen and traveled to the manger to worship their Savior and Lord.

The birth of Jesus was prophesied hundreds of years prior to the actual birth in Bethlehem.

Isaiah 9:6 reads, "For unto us a child is born, unto us a son is given: and the government shall be upon his shoulder: and his name shall be called Wonderful, Counselor, The mighty God, The everlasting Father, The Prince of Peace."

Angels did appear before many for the purpose of delivering an important message about God's plan. A great celebration was taking place in heaven with God's Son being born in Bethlehem. This birth was the greatest gift man would ever receive. This birth would allow man to receive life ev-erlasting through faith in Jesus Christ. Great joy and love was given to all of mankind. Countless numbers of angels were singing and praising God for His love and the birth of His Son.

We share this great joy and love with all those who are open to hearing God's word.

Mark 1:14–15 reads, "Now after that John was put in prison, Jesus came into Galilee, preaching the gospel of the kingdom of God. And say-ing, The time is fulfilled, and the kingdom of God is at hand: repent ye, and believe the gospel."

Jesus began his ministry in Galilee by telling all of humanity to repent from all of their sin and to believe and place all of their trust in Him and His message. Sometime later Jesus taught all of humanity how to pray.

Matthew 6:9–13 reads, "After this manner therefore pray ye: Our Father which art in heaven, Hallowed be thy name. Thy kingdom come. Thy will be done in earth, as it is in heaven. Give us this day our daily bread. And forgive us our debts, as we forgive our debtors. And lead us not into temptation, but deliver us from evil: For thine is the kingdom, and the power, and the glory, for ever, Amen."

Jesus' message is clear that His kingdom is near and humanity needs to be prepared. These prayers are to conform to His plans and will. God is in control and He will not tempt us more than what we are able to handle. He knows our every thought and knows what we need. The confession of sin and the asking of forgiveness is a daily requirement for all of humanity. Those that refuse to forgive the sins committed by others against them may experience God withholding His forgiveness. In other words, how we treat others will be reflected in how God blesses us.

Testing of Jesus

THE TESTING OF JESUS was a message to all of mankind that Jesus knows and has experienced all the tests and trials that mankind will ever encounter. Jesus was God and fully man. He was tested for the purpose of being prepared by God as the perfect sacrifice in washing away the sins of the world.

After the baptism of Jesus, the Holy Spirit led Jesus into the wilderness for forty days and nights. It was during this time that the devil tempted Jesus and tested Him by offering great wealth if He would worship Satan.

Matthew 4:11 reads, "Then the devil leaveth him, and, behold, angels came and ministered unto him."

Satan was allowed to test Jesus and place Him in difficult situations. This treatment by Satan was intense and involved three attempts to make Jesus use his divine powers.

Angels did comfort Jesus by providing peace and resolved many issues that needed attention.

God is in control and will at times allow Satan to test us or may allow some other evil into our lives. Man is often tempted by the world and may live a life that is not Christ centered. Prayer and study of the Bible will open the doors to spiritual strength that will defeat the world's temptations of pride, greed and lust.

Psalm 91:11 reads, "For he shall give his angels charge over thee, to keep thee in all thy ways."

Luke 4:10 reads, "For it is written, He shall give His angels charge over thee, to keep thee."

Angels are part of the believer's life and are always present to provide protection and comfort. Our daily lives as Christians are often confronted by evil and those who perpetuate evil.

We do not know the mind of God nor do we understand why he allows certain things to enter into our lives. However, we do know God is a loving, merciful, and a jealous God. He is all powerful and is able to pour out great blessings or unleash great torment. He is a just God who will not allow you to experience more temptation then you are able to handle. We trust in a God who is omnipotent, omniscient, omnipresent, and we rely on His great wisdom and direction.

Exodus 23:20 reads, "Behold, I send an angel before thee, to keep thee in the way, and to bring thee into the place which I have prepared."

Hebrews 1:14 reads, "Are they not all ministering spirits, sent forth to minister for them who shall be heirs of salvation."

The Christian is at the center of God's creation and he will be crowned with the honor and glory of salvation. We are on a journey throughout our lifetime that will include a number of tests, experiences and blessings that will prepare us to meet our Lord and Creator.

The gift of salvation was made possible for all of mankind through the death of God's only Son, Jesus Christ. This sacrifice opened the doors for all of mankind to receive eternal life by simply praying a simple prayer asking Jesus to enter into a person's life. Millions of people have been given the opportunity to pray this simple pray, but millions have refused. Those that received Jesus will spend eternity in heaven with their Lord and Savior, and those that rejected Jesus and refused to pray this simple prayer will spend eternity in Hell with Satan.

Prior to the birth and death of Jesus man was given the opportunity to believe in the one and only God the Father. God the Father commands man not to have any other Gods as found in Exodus.

Garden of Gethsemane

The Garden of Gethsemane is the place where Jesus prayed before being arrested, tried, and crucified. Jesus was both God and fully man. In this garden Jesus reveals his humanity as he expresses His fear and asks God that this cup would be removed from Him. However, after an evening of prayer Jesus ultimately becomes obedient to God's word and submits to God's will.

As Jesus prayed in the Garden of Gethsemane an angel appeared for the purpose of comforting Him.

Luke 22:42–44 reads, "Saying, Father, if thou be willing, remove this cup from me: nevertheless not my will, but thine, be done. And there appeared an angel unto him from heaven, strengthening him. And being in an agony he prayed more earnestly: and his sweat was as it were great drops of blood falling down to the ground."

Jesus spent that night in prayer and taking on the sins of the world. He was God's ultimate sacrifice for all of man's sin and needed to prepare himself to carry all of man's sin to the cross.

The message is that God knows our fears as part of the human race and will provide comfort and solace with our Father in a time of pain and suffering. Jesus knows the pain from betrayal as a kiss by Judas. Jesus knows the feelings of disappointment when He discovered friends had not kept watch, but had fallen asleep.

Jesus' reaction to those who arrested him was nonviolent even though He was completely innocent of any wrong doing. Jesus even healed the ear of Malchus when it was cut off by Peter with his razor sharp sword. Jesus was our living sacrifice which was offered by the Father as a payment for all the sins of mankind.

It is believed that angels are able to easily transition from the spiritual life to man's life on today's earth. In addition, man can be comforted by the Holy Spirit that lives within their earthly bodies and angels. Angels are

God's messengers and their sole purpose is to reflect His continue love for all of mankind.

Luke 16:22 reads, "And it came to pass, that the beggar died, and was carried by the angels into Abraham's bosom: the rich man also died, and was buried."

Angels are with us throughout this life and will carry us to our Lord and Savior at the end of this life. God lives within us through His Holy Spirit and has adopted us into His family.

Jesus could of had countless numbers of angels come to destroy His enemies and carry him to heaven. However, the fact is that there is a cost related to sin and Jesus was going to pay the cost for all the sins of mankind. There was no other way to pay for man's sins except a perfect sacrifice had to be made and that was the sinless life of Jesus.

Unfortunately, many will not believe and accept this free gift of eternal life. In addition, there are many who will not obey God's commands and will not ask for the forgiveness for their many sins. The Holy Spirit reveals to us our daily sins that need to be confessed to grow in faith.

Revelation 20:15, reads, "And whosoever was not found written in the book of life was cast into the lake of fire."

John 3:18 reads, "He that believeth on him is not condemned: but he that believeth not is condemned already, because he hath not believed in the name of the only begotten Son of God."

1 John 1:9 reads, "If we confess our sins, he is faithful and just to forgive us our sins, and to cleanse us from all unrighteousness."

Death of Jesus

THE SANHEDRIN ARRESTED, TRIED, and condemned Jesus for healing on the Sabbath, threatening to destroy the Jewish Temple using sorcery, and claiming to be the Son of God. Jesus was then taken to Pontius Pilate to be condemned for claiming to be King of the Jews. Pilate tries to release Jesus by providing another prisoner named Barabbas to take his place. The crowd insisted on having Jesus crucified.

God's angels were there prepared to act if needed. They were there in the Garden of Gethsemane to comfort and prepare Jesus for the crucifixion. They were at the tomb to roll away the stone and to explain to the Apostles and family what had happened to Jesus.

Luke 24:4–7 reads, "And it came to pass, as they were much perplexed thereabout, behold, two men stood by them in shining garments: And as they were afraid, and bowed down their faces to the earth, they said unto them, Why seek ye the living among the dead? He is not here, but is risen: remember how he spake unto you when he was yet in Galilee, Saying, The Son of man must be delivered into the hands of sinful men, and be crucified, and the third day rise again."

Man has been involved in sin since the beginning with Adam and Eve. God has blessed man and gave him free will and power over the things of the earth. Free will opened the doors and allowed man to freely choose between love and hate. Those who love God will freely follow His commands and show that love to others.

The cross is the door that opens to heaven. A man that comes to the cross will realize Jesus paid the price for all of man's sins and that He is waiting to welcome him to eternity.

The cross is there for all of mankind. Jesus' death on the cross and His resurrection triumphed over all evil and death. No matter how difficult the situation Jesus is standing at the door waiting to welcome all who have confessed their sins and believe to heaven.

1 John 1:9 reads, "If we confess our sins, he is faithful and just to forgive us our sins, and to cleanse us from all unrighteousness."

The way to heaven and eternal life is possible simply by praying a prayer of forgiveness, asking Jesus to enter your life, and turning the control of your life over to God. That simple prayer opens the door to eternal blessings, living in heaven for eternity, and the knowledge that these blessings are eternal. At the moment this prayer is completed the Holy Spirit enters a man's soul and communes with man's spirit. The Holy Spirit provides direction for man's life; inspires man's prayers, and provides insight into daily decisions. Living daily as a Christian requires direction from the Holy Spirit. A Christian loves God and strives to continually live a life that is obedient to God's commands.

Living a Christian Life

Becoming a Christian is easy for most people by simply praying a prayer in complete sincerity. However, there are some people who have a problem believing there is a God, there are some who believe in different gods, and still others refuse to believe in anything.

After the prayer of submission is completed the Holy Spirit enters a person's life and then all things are subject to change. The Holy Spirit will convict man of his many sins and the process of making changes and finding peace begins.

The Christian is a person that believes God created all things, the universe, heaven, and earth and all things that this includes. They also believe God sacrificed His only Son for all of man's sins so that they may experience eternal life in heaven.

A Christian begins by listening to God's word through Bible study and by recognizing all of the sins that exist in their life and striving to make a change. A Christian believes in heaven and hell and believes the penalty for sin is spiritual death.

Romans 6:23 reads, "For the wages of sin is death; but the gift of God is eternal life through Jesus Christ our Lord."

The gift from God is eternal spiritual life and the penalty for sin is eternal spiritual death. Faith in Jesus Christ sets the Christian free from the sin of this world and the enslavement of Satan and his many demons. Faith in God and His Son, Jesus Christ separates man from sin and allows man to freely live a life no longer enslaved by sin and death.

The priority and focus for the Christian's life is one that is centered by Holy Spirit in loving God and loving his neighbor. The Christian's love for God continues to grow in strength throughout his life.

2 Peter 3:18 reads, "But grow in grace, and in the knowledge of our Lord and Savior Jesus Christ. To him be glory both now and for ever. Amen."

The Christian's life is a life that is in constant growth and development, and increases in wisdom. As the Christian studies the Bible his soul and spirit are enriched with the comfort and peace of the Holy Spirit. The Christian prays daily for direction and for solution to all their concerns and problems. A Christian waits patiently for God's answers and trust in His direction.

Romans 8:11 reads, "But if the Spirit of him that raised up Jesus from the dead dwell in you, he that raised up Christ from the dead shall also quicken your mortal bodies by his Spirit that dwelleth in you."

The Holy Spirit that lives within a Christian is the same Holy Spirit that was indwelt within Jesus Christ. Therefore, it is a Christian's obligation to live a life that is controlled by the Holy Spirit. The Christian rejects his sinful nature and the morals and values of this world.

1 John 3:1–2 reads, "Behold, what manner of love the Father hath bestowed upon us, that we should be called the sons of God: therefore the world knoweth us not, because it knew him not. Beloved, now are we the sons of God, and it doth not yet appear what we shall be: but we know that, when he shall appear, we shall be like him; for we shall see him as he is."

1 John 3:6 reads, "Whosoever abideth in him sinneth not: whososever sinneth hath not seen him, neither know him."

The Christian is a child of God and is greatly loved by God. A person who continually lives in sin is a person who has never been transformed by God's life changing power.

Faith in Jesus

FAITH IN GOD AND His Son, Jesus Christ determines the eternal destiny for all of mankind. Those who have not seen Jesus and yet believe are blessed in a special way. The Angels were present with the disciples when Jesus ascended into heaven.

Acts 1:9–11 reads, "And when he had spoken these things, while they beheld, he was taken up; and a cloud received him out of their sight. And while they looked steadfastly toward heaven as he went up, behold, two men stood by them in white apparel; Which also said, Ye men of Galilee, why stand ye gazing up into heaven? this same Jesus which is taken up from you into heaven, shall so come in like manner as ye have seen him go into heaven."

Two angels in the form of men dressed in white explained to the disciples how Jesus will return to that very location (Mount of Olives) in the same way He ascended.

These disciples would receive God's Holy Spirit as Jesus promised. Jesus said He would ascend into heaven to prepare a place for them and He would leave the Holy Spirit with His indwelling presence and power.

John 14:16–17 reads, "And I will pray the Father, and he shall give you another Comforter, that he may abide with you for ever; Even the spirit of truth; whom the world cannot receive, because it seeth him not, neither knoweth him: but ye know him; for he dwelleth with you, and shall be in you."

The disciples were trained by Jesus and were instructed by angels to gain an understanding of what they were experiencing. Once Jesus ascended into heaven the Holy Spirit indwelled the souls of the disciples and taught each of them all things.

Angels are able to appear in human form and may not be immediately recognizable. This was obviously an extremely important event that needed the presence of angels to explain what was going to transpire. The disciples were all experiencing a number of divine moments that could cause a great deal of fear and confusion. These angels were able to explain to the disciples what they were seeing and bring to the disciples a sense of peace and divine glory.

1 Peter 1:21:23 reads, " Who by him do believe in God, that raised him up from the dead, and gave him glory; that your faith and hope might be in God. Seeing ye have purified your soul in obeying the truth through the Spirit unto unfeigned love of the brethren, see that ye love one another with a pure heart fervently: Being born again, not of corruptible seed, but of incorruptible seed, by the word of God, which liveth and abideth for ever."

This divine experience created within the disciples a faith that purified their souls and allowed them to love their brethren with a pure heart. The Holy Spirit also allows today's Christian to experience a saving faith that purifies their soul and grows in the love of his neighbor. The study of God's word with obedience to God's word produces love for your neighbor, the repentance of sin, and increases a desire to seek a closer walk with your Savior and experience spiritual growth.

Conscience

It is generally believed that each and every person is born with a conscience that makes a person aware of right and wrong. This conscience and how it interprets different situations and responds to different challenges could vary dramatically. For example, a person that grew up without a family and homeless may view stealing as a means of surviving from day to day. In addition, if this person is successful at stealing and does not experience any penalty for stealing they may attempt larger thefts. After years of stealing, their conscience may no longer be sensitive to the idea that stealing is wrong. Another example where a person's conscience may have been affected was during the great depression. People were forced to live with little or no money for food. These same people later may have become hoarders and greedy with little sympathy for the poor.

The numbing or deadening of the conscience is not only experienced in individuals but also by gangs, corporations, and in some cases governments. The continual reporting of daily casualties can be dismissed as the cost for achieving a successful goal. Another example as to where the conscience is numbed is when an individual is successful at achieving a certain social level of acceptance with bad behavior.

God created man with a soul, spirit, conscience, and body. The soul, spirit, and conscience lives forever and may influence a person's thoughts, actions, emotions, and sense of purpose.

However, God's word is the final authority and resource for making any decision.

Hebrews 4:12 reads, "For the word of God is quick, and powerful, and sharper than any twoedged sword, piercing even to the dividing asunder of soul and spirit, and of the joints and marrow, and is a discerner of the thoughts and intents of the heart."

The degree of purity within a man is determined by the relationship between a man's soul and spirit with God's Holy Spirit.

Titus 1:15 reads, "Unto the pure all things are pure: but unto them that are defiled and unbelieving is nothing pure; but even their mind and conscience is defiled."

Living a life as a Christian and following Christian teachings and principals requires a person who has a developed a strong relationship with his God and Savior. The conscience of an unbeliever is defiled and not able to reflect the teachings of the Holy Spirit.

Christian morals and teachings are under attack from many different countries, institutions, and organizations. Recently, Russia's military invaded Ukraine killing many men, women, and children. The invasion has caused a great deal of pain and suffering for millions of people. The reason given for the invasion by Vladimir Putin was that Ukraine belongs to Russia and is now a threat to Russia. The Russian military is systemically destroying thousands of homes and businesses in Ukraine making it impossible for the people of Ukraine to make a living and causing millions to flee for their lives. This barbaric approach to resolving a problem in 2022 seems unconscionable.

Meeting God

The Apostle Paul was a man who lived a life that was on the edge. He faced death throughout most of his life, traveled throughout the eastern Mediterranean area and preached to both the Jews and the Gentiles. He was stoned and beaten for his message and was shipwrecked and almost drowned.

However, he continued with God's strength under life threatening conditions, hatred, and illness. He understood and explained that this body we now possess will pass away and we will be given a new spiritual body.

1 Corinthians 15:51–52 reads, "Behold, I show you a mystery; We shall not all sleep, but we shall all be changed, In a moment, in the twinkling of an eye, at the last trump: for the trumpet shall sound, and the dead shall be raised incorruptible, and we shall be changed."

1 Thessalonians 4:16–17 reads, "For the Lord himself shall descend from heaven with a shout, with the voice of the archangel, and the trump of God: and the dead in Christ shall rise first. Then we which are alive and remain shall be caught up together with them in the clouds, to meet the Lord in the air: and so shall we ever be with the Lord."

During the Rapture all believers will be caught up in the air to meet their Lord. Those that have died will be raised from the grave and their souls and spirits will be given a new Christ- like body. The Archangel with God's great power will sound his trump that will raise all believers both dead and alive to meet their Lord and Savior in the sky.

Philippians 3:21 reads, "Who shall change our vile body, that it may be fashioned like unto his glorious body, according to the working whereby he is able even to subdue all things unto himself."

Christians will be given a glorified body that will reflect God's perfections and will no longer be limited by a body that is subject to sin and disease.

Christians will be judged for the life they lived and God will reward those who have made a difference in people lives. We as Christians have been redeemed at a very high price, the death of God's only Son. Christians remain on this earth for the purpose of bringing others into God's kingdom and proclaiming God's love and grace to all of mankind.

The time when the Rapture will occur is not known by any man. It is believed the first rapture occurred during Jesus resurrection.

Matthew 27:51–53 reads, "And, behold, the veil of the temple was rent in twain from the top to the bottom: and the earth did quake, and rocks rent; And the graves were opened; and many bodies of the saints which slept arose, And came out of the graves after his resurrection, and went into the holy city, and appeared unto many."

It is believed that the Apostle Matthew included this eye witness account for good reason. A great earthquake did occur that broke open many rocks of the graves of many Old Testament Saints. No doubt, the people of Jerusalem after seeing the saints of the past appear throughout the city came to the realization that Jesus was who he said he was, the Messiah, the Son of God. The veil that separated the Holy of Holies from common man was torn and common man now had direct access to God their creator. It is believed the Old Testament Saints were raised with Jesus during this time and were given new immortal bodies.

The Rapture will come as a thief in the night when man will least expect it. We need to be prepared and have our priorities in place.

It is believed that many angels will be involved in many different ways.

Angels Sound the Trumpets

It is believed that after the Rapture of the church is completed the tribulation will begin.

Matthew 24:3–8 reads, "And as he sat upon the mount of Olives, the disciples came unto him privately, saying, Tell us, when shall these things be? And what shall be the sign of thy coming, and of the end of the world? And Jesus answered and said unto them, Take heed that no man deceive you. For many shall come in my name, saying, I am Christ; and shall deceive many. And ye shall hear of wars and rumors of wars: see that ye be not troubled: for all these things must come to pass, but the end is not yet. For nations shall rise against nations, and kingdom against kingdom: and there shall be famines, and pestilences, and earthquakes, in divers places. All these are the beginning of sorrows."

Angels in heaven will be sounding the trumps of warning that the end is approaching.

Matthew 24:21 reads, "For then shall be great tribulation, such as was not since the beginning of the world to this time, no, nor ever shall be."

The message is that the final period of time for the earth will be marked by many earth quakes, destructive storms, suffering from disease, famine, and many other natural disasters. Many angels will be sounding the alarm that the end is near and people need to worship God and to live a life that follows God's commands.

We are all experiencing the effects of climate change as the earth's atmosphere becomes warmer and creates an increase in the number of severe hurricanes, earth quakes, floods, draughts, and famines. Man was given a perfect and beautiful earth to care for and manage. However, man has polluted the earth's atmosphere with the burning of fossil fuels and left the earth with large open pits. Man has also polluted the oceans with the dumping of millions of tons of garbage killing off millions of fish and other sea creatures. Some governments actually allow the dumping of raw sewage into their lakes that are used for drinking water. The examples of bad decision made in the care and management of the earth and its atmosphere appears to be endless. Many of the issues facing man today are self-inflicted and caused by greed.

However, God will protect the genuine believer and rapture them from the earth before the Tribulation period.

Revelation 3:10 reads, "Because thou hast kept the word of my patience, I also will keep thee from the hour of temptation, which shall come upon all the world, to try them that dwell upon the earth."

The genuine believer will be caught up in the clouds with the Lord.

1 Thessalonians 4:13–18 reads, "But I would not have you to be ignorant, brethren, concerning them which are asleep, that ye sorrow not, even as others which have no hope. For if we believe that Jesus died and rose again, even so them also which sleep in Jesus will God bring with him. For this we say unto you by the word of the Lord, that we which are alive and remain unto the coming of the Lord shall not prevent them which are asleep. For the Lord himself shall descend from heaven with a shout, with the voice of the archangel, and with the trump of God: and the dead in Christ shall rise first: Then we which are alive and remain shall be caught up together with them in the clouds, to meet the Lord in the air: and so shall we ever be with the Lord. Wherefore comfort one another with these words."

The Holy Spirit

THE HOLY SPIRIT'S SUPERNATURAL power opens the eyes of man to the realization of God's gracious gift of eternal life. Man on his own is dead in his sin and blind to the power and the magnitude of God's love for all of mankind. The Holy Spirit will change a person by producing a Christ-like character within a person. Consequently, a person that has become a Christian will become highly sensitive to sin and will avoid sin whenever possible. Some sin is extremely dangerous and is impossible to escape without experiencing some mental and physical damage. Any sexual encounter outside the marriage between a man and woman is sin.

1 Corinthians 6:18–20 reads, "Fee fornication. Every sin that a man doeth is without the body; but he that committeth fornication sinneth against his own body. What? Know ye not that your body is the temple of the Holy Ghost which is in you, which ye have of God, and ye are not your own? For ye are bought with a price: therefore glorify God in your Body, and in your spirit, which are God's."

1 Peter 5:8–9 reads, "Be sober, be vigilant; because your adversary the devil, as a roaring lion, walketh about, seeking whom he may devour:

We are in a daily battle with Satan and his demons. He is extremely powerful and cunning, capable of defeating and inflecting great damage to the strongest and best prepared Christian. However, God has promised us not to test us more then what we are able to handle.

1 Corinthians 10:13 reads, "There hath no temptation taken you but such as is common to man: but God is faithful, who will not suffer you to be tempted above that ye are able; but will with the temptation also make a way to escape, that ye may be able to bear it."

Satan will actually attack innocent children, try to destroy the family unit, and introduce questionable topics in children's text books. In addition, millions of dollars are spent each year trying to pass new laws for the purpose of changing the definition of the family. People who are involved in sin will try to convince others that there nothing wrong with living in sin. They will spend millions of dollars on research projects trying to prove that there is nothing wrong with their sinful actions. The Bible is very clear on the definition of the family unit.

Satan can easily confuse people in believing there is nothing wrong in living a life filled with sin. The TV and other computer networks are filled with countless sinful messages. Many of these sinful messages are directed at children. Christians are able to test these messages of sin by reviewing the final result.

Matthew 7:16–17 reads, "Ye shall know them by their fruits. Do men gather grapes of thorns, or figs of thistles? Even so every good tree bringeth forth good fruit ; but a corrupt tree bringeth forth evil fruit."

God, as the gardener will cut down the trees that do not produce good fruit. Those individuals who continue to live a life filled with sin will continue to be an adversary and create conflict.

We Will All Be Accountable

OUR UNDERSTANDING OF GOD and how He works in our daily life is limited. The Apostles after three years of intense training by Jesus had limited understanding of how Jesus would defeat death and forgive all of man's sin.

Acts 1:11 reads, "Which also said, Ye men of Galilee, why stand ye gazing up into heaven? this same Jesus, which is taken up from you into heaven, shall so come in like manner as ye have seen him go into heaven."

In this situation an angel explains in detail how Jesus will return during His second coming. This message is still repeated today as Christians throughout the world prepare for their Savior and Lord's second coming.

Revelation 1:7 reads, "Behold, he cometh with clouds; and every eye shall see him, and they also which pierced him: and all kindred of the earth shall wail because of him. Even so, Amen."

Countless number of angels will be present with Jesus during His second coming. These angels will fill a number of various important needs. Many will be singing praises and worshiping the Almighty God, the Creator of all and Savior of the world. Many others will be involved in the judgment of mankind and the lives that they lived.

Revelations 20:11–13 reads, "And I saw a great white throne, and him that sat on it, from whose face the earth and the heaven fled away; and thee was found no place for them. And I saw the dead, small and great, stand before God; and the books were opened: and another book was opened, which is the book of life: and the dead were judged out of those things which were written in the books, according to their works. And the sea gave up the dead which were in it; and death and hell delivered up the dead which were in them: and they were judged every man according to their works."

The Bible tells us that the Son of Man will send millions and millions of angels that will gather all the nations, and will separate them one from another as a shepherd separates the sheep from the goats. The Son of Man will also change our human bodies to be like his glorified body.

There will be two books, one that details the life of those that rejected any belief in God and one that contains the names of all those that accepted eternal life with faith in God. This will be the final judgment.

Message of Love For Mankind

ALL OF GOD'S MESSENGERS both angels and humans exhibited great love for God and mankind as they have lived their lives in submission to God's direction. Moses' message for the Israelites was God's love and compassion as He released the Israelites from their bondage and directed them to the Promised Land. God's love was also fulfilled as He molded Moses into a great leader of the Israelites. It was The Apostle James' desire and love for God's people that allowed him to deliver such fiery sermons that those that were in ear shot were moved and recognized that he was speaking of God's truth. The Apostle Peter's love for Jesus was unquestionable. Among the Apostles, Peter was the first in many ways to express his love for Jesus. He was the first to recognize Jesus as the Messiah and the Savior for all mankind. Peter was impetuous and his love for Jesus was obvious as he jumped into the water because he could not wait for the boat to arrive. The Apostle Peter made many mistakes, but Jesus loved him regardless. When Jesus asked Peter three times if he loved him he was devastated. And, when a broken Peter said yes, Jesus said, feed my sheep. The Apostle Peter spent the remainder of his 40 years feeding Jesus' sheep showing his love for both His Lord and neighbor. The Apostle John was a man that Jesus loved for his ability to grasp the importance of biblical truths and teachings. John was a compassionate man and had a heart for those in need.

John 13:1 reads, "Now before the feast of the Passover, when Jesus knew that his hour was come that he should depart out of this world unto the Father, having loved his own which were in the world, he loved them unto the end."

No greater love has ever been seen as when God gave his only Son. No greater humility has ever been experienced as when God's only Son became a servant and teacher to his people. And, finally Jesus' obedience, death, and Resurrection revealed a love that defeated death and opened the door to everlasting life.

God has given to us many messages of love for us to follow. God's messengers all understood the importance of listening and understanding God's word and direction. Moses and Elijah were completely dependent on God for their daily existence. Peter, James, and John were also dependent on God as they preached God's word in a hostile environment where death was a possibility any day. All these men loved their neighbors and were all willing to make the ultimate sacrifice so that they may experience eternal life with their Creator.

We need to remember that the greatest gift is God's love for us and we need to share that gift with our neighbors. There is nothing we could do that would have a greater impact on their lives than to explain the way of salvation. The consequence of this decision is life or death and will last for eternity. Unfortunately, many churches are adrift today and spend more time speaking of social issues and in some cases nothing about salvation. We all need to be prepared to answer the question, have you fed my sheep? What kind of shepherd have you been for God's people? Have you been loving, caring, and thoughtful of others? Have you been willing to be protective of others from the wolves of this world, are you willing to give a helping hand to others, and are you willing to go after the one that is lost?

Message of Spiritual Joy

THE MESSAGE OF SPIRITUAL joy is the fact that the amount of spiritual joy we experience is determined by how we live our lives and share God's love with others. The amount of spiritual joy we experience in our daily lives is controlled by the Holy Spirit within our being. The Holy Spirit communes with us in ways we cannot understand and intercedes for us in our prayers. Unfortunately, the degree and consistency of spiritual joy within our life is affected by our sin. Sin has a lasting and immediate effect on our spirit and soul and will quench the spirit and diminish our spiritual joy.

The degree of spiritual joy will fluctuate and will react to highly spiritual music, preaching, or other messages of God's love and compassion. It is not uncommon for people to be overcome by Spiritual Joy. Another source of spiritual joy is from others in a prayer group or church service.

Hebrews 10:24–25 reads, "And let us consider one another to provoke unto love and to good works: Not forsaking the assembling of ourselves together, as the manner of some is; but exhorting one another: and so much the more, as ye see the day approaching."

The purpose of assembly is to primarily worship and praise the Creator of all things, our great and Almighty God. We love and cherish this time we spend together encouraging each other in resolving life's challenges. We share our concerns and pray for each individual and their unique needs and situation.

As Moses, we need to consider all of God's blessings and realize that He is the one and only God and the Creator of all. Moses had great spiritual joy when he saw what God had done for the Israelites.

Exodus 15:1–5 reads, "Then sang Moses and the children of Israel this song unto the Lord, and spake, saying, I will sing unto the Lord, for he hath triumphed gloriously: the horse and his rider hath he thrown into the sea. The Lord is my strength and song, and he become my salvation: he is my

God, and I will prepare him a habitation; my father's God, and I will exalt him. The Lord is man of war: the Lord is his name. Pharaoh's chariots and his host hath he cast into the sea: his chosen captains also are drowned in the Red Sea. The depths have covered them: they sank into the bottom as a stone."

Moses and the Israelites sang a song of great joy and praise knowing that the hand of the Lord had protected them from Pharaoh's army and certain death and slavery. We know that the Creator of the universe with His mighty powers and with greatness of majesty is our personal Lord and Savior and that He has placed His hand of protection over us each day. He is with us daily and directs us away from the Pharaoh's of this world. Our hearts are full of spiritual joy as we sing and praise our Lord and Savior. We fall on our faces as we ask for redemption from our pride of life and our sin nature.

Elijah was a man who wrestled with his expectations for how events should unfold. It wasn't until he realized that God was in control regardless of his own expectations that he was able to fully understand and appreciate the sweet comfort of spiritual joy. God is in control as to how events unfold in our daily lives. We are responsible for being obedient to God's word, to submit our requests in prayer, and to be faithful in all things. We rest in Him putting all of our trust in Him knowing He loves us and is preparing our way.

2 Corinthians 5:5–7 reads, "Now he that hath wrought us for the self-same thing is God, who also hath given unto us the earnest of the spirit. Therefore we are always confident, knowing that, whilst we are at home in the body, we are absent from the Lord. For we walk by faith, not by sight."

Rejoice in the Lord Always

Our souls long to be with our Creator and Lord. And, our souls jump with joy as we experience spiritual joy when we hear His words in song, in testimony, and in reading. Our spiritual joy increases as we learn to view our life in its proper perspective. We need to focus on the final goal and prepare ourselves for an eternal life with our Lord and Savior.

Romans 5:3–5 reads, "And not only so, but we glory in tribulations also: knowing that tribulation worketh patience; And patience, experience; and experience, hope: And hope maketh not ashamed; because the love of God is shed abroad in our hearts by the Holy Ghost which is given unto us."

The Apostle Paul realized that growth in faith was only possible by living through trials. Trials are designed by God specifically for each individual to improve each Christian's character. God's plan for each individual was established before their birth into this world and is dependent on decisions made by each individual to accept or reject God's gift of eternal life through His only Son, Jesus Christ.

Trails may bring temporary grief. However, the deep living joy that lives within a Christian's soul is based upon God's grace.

1 Peter 1:6 reads, "Wherein ye greatly rejoice, though now for a season, if need be, ye are in heaviness through manifold temptations."

When we succeed against temptations we grow in faith and we experience spiritual joy. Faith grows stronger when tested with trials and temptations and we finally realize we can always put our faith in the Lord to carry us through any situation.

God changed Peter from a selfish, self-centered man with many frailties into a spirit-filled vessel capable of healing those with infirmities. Peter's spiritual joy was experienced with trials and struggles knowing God was pruning away his sinful nature.

1 Peter 4:13 reads, "But rejoice, inasmuch as ye are partakers of Christ's sufferings; that, when his glory shall be revealed, ye may be glad also with exceeding joy."

1 Peter 1:7 reads, "That the trial of your faith, being much more precious than of gold that perisheth, though it be tried with fire, might be found unto praise and honor and glory at the appearing of Jesus Christ."

We run a race with countless numbers of angels in heaven cheering us on as we strengthen our endurance and conquer each new challenge. We are waiting to hear the words, "well done my good and faithful servant."

Matthew 25:21 reads, "His Lord said unto him, Well done, thou good and faithful servant: thou hast been faithful over a few things, I will make thee ruler over many things: enter thou into the joy of thy Lord."

The Apostle James' (Son of Thunder) spiritual joy was amazing. He was the oldest Apostle and one of the most spiritually mature with a gift for speaking. His heart was fixed on delivering the message of salvation to all who would listen and his spiritual joy was increased as new believers made decisions to follow the teaching of Jesus the Messiah.

Philippians 4:4 reads, "Rejoice in the Lord always: and again I say, Rejoice.'

Rejoice in God's Blessings

The Apostle John (the beloved disciple) was an Apostle whose life was centered on his love for His Lord and Savior and his love for his neighbor.

1 John 1:4 reads, "And these things write we unto you, that your joy may be full."

John was sharing his personal experience of knowing his Lord and Savior and the joy that it brought him each day. John's joy was due to the fact his entire life was centered on God and his relationship with God. Consequently, his joy was not affected by circumstances or by the increase or decrease of possessions, prestige, reputation, or any other earthly pleasure. His joy was directly related to having the Holy Spirit fill him each day with joy as he praised and thanked God for his many blessings and continued to minister to God's people and the church.

Today the world and man are driven by expectations and how to achieve the next goal of wealth, possession, or position. The Apostle John and the other Apostles achieved spiritual joy by furthering the gospel and building the church. Our joy is also achieved by furthering the gospel and seeing how God's kingdom is expanded with each new soul.

Luke 15: 4–7 reads, "What man of you, having a hundred sheep, if he lose one of them, doth not leave the ninety and nine in the in wilderness, and go after that which is lost, until he find it? And when he hath found it, he layeth it on his shoulders, rejoicing. And when he cometh home, he calleth together his friends and neighbors, saying unto them, rejoice with me; for I have found my sheep which was lost. I say unto you, that likewise joy shall be in heaven over one sinner that repenteth, more than over ninety and nine just persons, which need no repentance."

Man is God's creation and is of more value then we can comprehend. The purpose of the church is to care for and nourish the souls that attend and to search for those that are lost. Our churches should be focused on the conversion of those that have not made the decision to follow Jesus' teachings. Our church services should be filled with testimonies of those that have surrendered their life to Christ and have made a change in their life. The members of the church need to be experiencing spiritual joy along with those in heaven as testimonies are told of the lives that have been changed. We were created for the purpose of praising God for His unbelievable gifts and blessings.

God's message to the believer is that He is watching over them, protecting them, and providing them a peace that they cannot explain.

Philippians 4:6–7 reads, "Be careful for nothing; but in everything by prayer and supplication with thanksgiving let your requests be made known unto God. And the peace of God, which passeth all understanding, shall keep your hearts and minds through Christ Jesus."

God is in control and there is no reason to worry. It is the believer's responsibility to bring all of his concerns to God in prayer. And, to bring all of his prayers of concerns with thanksgiving for the blessings he has received. It is important that we realize all that we are or ever will be is from God's love, mercy, and grace.

Blessings Poured Into Our Heart

God's love is never ending and is poured out through His Holy Spirit into our hearts. Most people do not comprehend the depth and never ending love of God.

We are to be fully engaged in taking advantage of our personal relationship with our Creator to experience the full impact of His peace and grace in our daily life. His peace and grace gives us the knowledge to break free from the world and all of it's evil desires and lusts. The world and it's obsession with wealth is extremely dangerous and will cause men to kill, steal, and destroy entire families. In some ways, the desire for wealth is like an addictive drug that will take control of every decision. This addiction will dictate standards for ethics, morals, and how men view his neighbor.

Romans 5:1–2 reads, "Therefore being justified by faith, we have peace with God through our Lord Jesus Christ. By whom also we have access by faith into this grace wherein we stand, and rejoice in hope of the glory of God."

We have been justified by our faith in the Lord Jesus Christ. Jesus Christ paid the price for us to enjoy the great peace that is available to all that have faith. As we travel through this journey of life we need to rejoice in all of God's blessings and rest in the peace that is beyond our understanding.

1 Peter 5:6–7 reads, "Humble yourselves therefore under the mighty hand of God, that he may exalt you in due time. Casting all your cares upon him; for he careth for you."

Our life has been turned over to God and His will. We wait and act in complete humility and prayer looking and listening for His direction and will for our life. We need to remember all those who have been martyred, those that have sacrificed everything, and the ultimate gift of God's only Son. We need to approach our Savior and Lord on our knees in complete humility.

The Holy Spirit is part of the Trinity and at the same time a separate entity within the same Deity. He is also called the great Comforter because of the Holy Spirit's ability to provide peace to people when they are under severe conflict, pain, and suffering. The peace that is provided by the Holy Spirit is a very unique peace that only the Holy Spirit is able to provide.

John 14:26–27 reads, "But the Comforter, which is the Holy Ghost, whom the Father will send in my name, he shall teach you all things, and bring all things to your remembrance, whatsoever I have said unto you. Peace I leave with you, my peace I give unto you: not as the world giveth, give I unto you. Let not your heart be troubled, neither let it be afraid."

The believer receives the glorious gift of the Holy Spirit when a decision is made and a confession of faith is declared. This is the same Holy Spirit that Peter received at Pentecost that allowed him to preach with such conviction that over 3,000 were baptized and converted to following Jesus' teachings. Most believers do not realize the power of the Holy Spirit within their life. The believer that is obedient to God's commands, has placed their full faith in our loving God, and is thankful for all of God's blessings will experience the peace of the Holy Spirit. The Holy Spirit is able to provide many blessings, such as confidence, the appropriate words in a difficult situation, love, compassion, and awareness of others situations, open opportunities that would not otherwise be available, and bringing people into your life for support and perspective. These are just a few of the blessings associated with living a life that allows the Holy Spirit to take up residence within your life and gives you God's peace.

Colossians 1:20 reads, "And, having made peace through the blood of his cross, by him to reconcile all things unto himself: by him, I say, whether they be things in earth, or things in heaven."

Peace of God

God's peace that was given to sinful man was only possible because of Jesus' sacrifice and His blood that was shed on the cross. The believer receives this peace daily because of the Holy Spirit's continual intercession for us as we struggle with daily challenges due to our weaknesses and temptations. This peace is God's peace and cannot be explained by man.

Psalm 139: 1–6 reads, "O Lord thou hast searched me, and know me. Thou knowest my downsitting, and mine upraising; thou understandest my thoughts afar off. Thou compassest my path and my lying down, and art acquainted with all my ways. For there is not a word in my tongue, but, lo, O Lord, thou knows it altogether. Thou hast beset me behind and before, and laid thine hand upon me. Such knowledge is too wonderful for me; it is high, I cannot attain unto it."

As believers we place our complete trust in Jesus, we place Him at the center of our life, and wait patiently under His peace for His direction. Only God knows the true way for our life and we need to surrender to His direction. His path for our lives has been prepared and we need to walk under his protection.

The Apostle John was a man of Jesus' love and peace.

John 20:19–22 reads, "Then the same day at evening, being the first day of the week, when the doors were shut where the disciples were assembled for fear of the Jews, came Jesus and stood in the midst, and saith unto them, Peace be unto you. And when he had so said, he showed unto them his hands and his side. Then were the disciples glad, when they saw the Lord. Then said Jesus to them again, Peace be unto you: as my Father hath sent me, even so send I you. And when he had said this, he breathed on them, and saith unto them, Receive ye the Holy Ghost."

The Apostle John and others were meeting behind locked doors in fear not knowing if they would be the next to be arrested and possibly crucified. The miraculous appearance of Jesus in this room gave the disciples the peace that passes all understanding. This type of peace erased all doubt, established confidence, and fulfilled their faith. They were in fact vessels that were now prepared to receive the Holy Spirit. At this point, the Holy Spirit was able to transform each of the disciples and work with them individually to carry out God's plan. At some time later, all believers were baptized by the Holy Spirit at Pentecost and were sent out speaking many different languages.

The Apostle John understood the meaning of peace and spoke of peace to the churches he ministered.

John 16:33 reads, "These things I have spoken unto you, that in me ye might have peace. In the world ye shall have tribulation: but be of good cheer; I have overcome the world."

Believers have made a decision to follow Jesus Christ and His teachings and are therefore walking with the Holy Spirit in God's plan. However, believers are still in this world and pressured by Satan and his demons. The Apostle John in this verse was reminding these believers to be at peace in knowing God is in control and he has beaten evil at every step. As believers we are to rest in God's grace knowing our sins were forgiven by the sacrifice of God's only Son.

God's Plan

As NATURAL MEN WE have many frailties and a fallen nature that invades our daily life with many distractions that are destructive to living a Christ centered life.

John 14: 27 reads, "Peace I leave with you, my peace I give unto you: not as the world giveth, give I unto you. Let not your heart be troubled, neither letit be afraid."

We are bombarded each day by a world that has a set of morals and ethics that are based on pleasure, pride of life, and greed. As our society continues to crumble with no moral or ethical guide, our leadership does not provide any type of direction for reversing a path to civil anarchy. The lack of respect for another person, the sense of entitlement, and the act of killing another person for no reason is the result of a society without values or morals.

We see this lack of self-respect and love for our neighbor in the daily news as men and women kill each other for money and possessions.

The peace that a believer receives is not from the world or from anything that is related to the world. Peace from God is not related to wealth, pleasure, or any other aspect of worldly living. A believer's peace comes from knowing that they are living in God's will, they have eternal security, God will provide for their needs, and God will direct them as to which path to follow.

A natural man (e.g., carnal man, fallen man) is a man that is completely dependent on physical things and unable to receive and preserve spiritual blessings from the Holy Spirit. A natural man is completely possessed by physical desires, senses of pleasures, taste, touch, emotions, pride of life, and ego. He is controlled by his eyes and heart as he lusts for evil, for status, and wealth.

1 Corinthians 2:14 reads, "But the natural man received not the things of the spirit of God: for they are foolishness unto him: neither can he know them, because they are spiritually discerned."

A natural man takes on many of the characteristics of Satan and his demons as he goes through life self absorbed and dispensing evil to those that get in his way. The soul and spirit of the natural man escapes into a deep hibernation and can only be awaken by the Holy Spirit.

The spiritual man knows the voice of the Lord and is able to experience peace knowing he is in God's will.

John 10:3–5 reads, "To him the porter openeth; and the sheep hear his voice: and he calleth his own sheep by name, and leadeth them out. And when he putteth forth his own sheep, he goeth before them, and the sheep follow him: for they know his voice. And a stranger will they not follow, but will fee from him: for they know not the voice of strangers."

God calls each individual by name and leads them through their life. God's leading is obvious when people look back over their life and see how God has open doors, changed events, and used others to lead or change their attitude.

To grow in our faith we need to realize that the goals and values of the world are not God's goals and values. His direction for our life may not be what we want for our life. And, to hear God's voice requires us to change how we think and to train our minds to close out the noise of the world and to allow His Spirit to take control of our thoughts. God speaks to each of us throughout each day.

Listening to God

THE HOLY SPIRIT COMMUNES with the spiritual man in ways that are not understood by the natural man. The Holy Spirit acts as a conduit between man and God as He creates ideas and impressions within a spiritual man's life. These thoughts and impressions are given frequently throughout each day to man for developing ideas and impressions. The gift of the Holy Spirit to a spiritual man brings great peace, joy, and allows him to rejoice in the knowledge he is in God's will. A spiritual man's life has purpose and that purpose is following God's direction.

The natural man worships his possessions and all other things and has stopped his soul and spirit from functioning. Sin and Satan has blinded the natural man and caused him to consider worshiping God as foolishness.

1 Kings 19:12 reads, "And after the earthquake a fire, but the Lord was not in the fire: and after the fire a still small voice."

Elijah, a spiritual man, was able to hear this still small voice. Elijah's heart and mind knew God's voice and was able to recognize that it was God speaking to him. It is when we are silent and separated from the world our spirit begins to hear and recognize God's thoughts and impressions. The thoughts we receive from our spirit are not like most thoughts. They are like whispers that are easily forgotten in a manner of minutes. In most cases they need to be written down before they are lost.

Proverbs 24:3–4 reads, "Through wisdom is a house builded; and by understanding it, is established. And by knowledge shall the chambers be filled with all precious and pleasant riches."

Every person has a spirit and soul; however few people understand it or know how to care for it. The natural man has a mind that is completely consumed by thoughts and ideas based on the world's values and ethics. In most cases any thought of a spiritual nature is immediately discarded. The natural man's mind is at war with the spiritual and will drown out any spiritual thought or distract the mind with other thoughts. Controlling your thoughts or selecting thoughts is difficult and requires God's strength and direction.

Isaiah 11:2 reads, "And the spirit of the Lord shall rest upon him, the spirit of wisdom and understanding, the spirit of counsel and might, the spirit of knowledge and the fear of the Lord."

Most people need to set aside some time each day to be at peace with God's word and allow the Holy Spirit to commune with their spirit. In prayer we praise His name, thank Him for the gift of His Son and His many daily blessings, ask for forgiveness for our many sins, and submit our requests and concerns. We need to be at rest to allow our spirit and mind to focus on what is really a priority.

Endurance and Patience

God's plan for mankind and how He unfolds His plan is only known to God. Generally, we are able to see God's plans as we look back over many years. It is only when we come to the realization and understanding that God is in control that are we able to turn over all of our concerns to God and experience God's peace.

We are all at times placed in situations where we need to be patient and endure difficulties. As we go through these circumstances we begin to develop strength and are better able to endure persecution. The growing in faith and communing with the Holy Spirit is directly related to developing patience and endurance in difficult situations. It is extremely important that we allow the Holy Spirit to take control in difficult situations. The Holy Spirit is able to carry us through difficult times and to provide a resting place for our emotions and mind. Some of us go through a lifetime of difficult situations and have survived simply by turning over all fear, hate, and sin in prayer to God.

Ephesians 3:10–15 reads, "To the intent that now unto the principalities and powers in heavenly places might be known by the church the manifold wisdom of God. According to the eternal purpose which he purposed in Christ Jesus our Lord: In whom we have boldness and access with confidence by the faith of him. Wherefore I desire that ye faint not at my tribulations for you, which is your glory. For this cause I bow my knees unto the Father of our Lord Jesus Christ. Of whom the whole family in heaven and earth is named."

We are a member of a family of believers that number in the millions that are both in heaven and on earth. All of these members have derived their faith from God our Creator and He now counts each one of us as His own.

The Jewish people suffered greatly for hundreds of years as slaves under the barbaric rule of the Egyptians until God called Moses to lead them to the Promised Land. Even then the Jewish people suffered as they wandered the desert for 40 years because of lack of faith and the sin of building pagan gods. God strengthened Moses and gave Moses the endurance to experience the longsuffering of leading over 600,000 people through the desert.

Exodus 34:5–6 reads, "And the Lord descended in the cloud, and stood with him there, and proclaimed the name of the Lord. And the Lord passed by before him, and proclaimed, The Lord, The Lord God, merciful and gracious, long-suffering, and abundant in goodness and truth."

God is merciful and patient with us as we struggle with sin in a world that is lost in the pride of life, distorted values, and the refusal to recognize all of God's blessings.

Psalm 103:7–14 reads, "He made known his ways unto Moses, his acts unto the children of Israel. The Lord is merciful and gracious, slow to anger, and plenteous in mercy. He will not always chide: neither will he keep his anger forever. He hath not dealt with us after our sins, nor rewarded us according to our iniquities. For as the heavens is high above the earth, so great is his mercy toward them that fear him. As far as the east is from the west, so far hath he removed our transgressions from us. Like as a father pitieth his children, so the Lord pitieth them that fear him. For he knoweth our frame; he remembereth that we are dust."

God was slow to anger with both Moses and the Israelites; he is merciful, patient, and gives us time to repent of our sins. We need to approach our Lord and Savior with a contrite heart, with weeping, asking for forgiveness and asking for His mercy.

The Family

TODAY, THE FAMILY IS under attack from all directions. Satan's primary goal is to destroy all of God's creation including all of mankind and the church. The methods and strategies he uses are very clever and are not normally recognized by man. Recently, there has been a push by special interest groups and lawmakers to change the definition of the family. This proposal would change the definition of the family to include any grouping of people.

Science and medical research has now made it possible for people to change their sex from man to woman or women to man. This has resulted in some people actually claiming not to be of any sex. These changes will have a major impact on the mental health of the world. Most men and women place great importance on being able to identify with their sexual role within the family. Most women place great importance on being able to have children and have an active role in raising them to adulthood. The bond that is created between a mother and a child is paramount in ensuring that a child has a healthy perspective of self and a healthy respect for others. Those children that are not able to develop a strong bond between themselves and a parent will search for that bond in other places.

This attack on the family will have a major impact on the mental health of the world. Special interest groups are actively introducing new laws that will introduce young children to the idea that the family is not composed of a father, mother, and sisters and brothers.

The Bible is full of examples how God works with and protects families after falling into very difficult situations. One example, is the life of Joseph and how he was able to survived after being sold by his brothers because of jealousy to a caravan. In God's grand plan Joseph would end up working in Egypt for the Pharaoh.

Genesis 45:7–8 reads, "And God sent me before you to preserve you a posterity in the earth, and to save your lives by a great deliverance. So now it was not you that sent me hither, but God: and he hath made me a father to Pharaoh, and Lord of all his house, and a ruler throughout all the land of Egypt."

Joseph understood how God worked in his life and that he was in Egypt to prepare for the famine and to prepare for his father, Jacob and his brothers. Joseph with God's help was able to forgive his brothers for selling him and for their jealousy. Joseph did not harbor hatred or vengeance in his mind and soul, but was able to push past these poisonous ideas and feelings. Your soul needs to be clear of ideas and feelings that could prevent the Holy Spirit full access to your soul and hamper future blessings.

God loves the family just as Christ loves the family. The marriage between the husband and wife provides a safe place where a child can learn what means to be loved and how to love others. There are enormous benefits to be realized by children from living in a loving and nurturing family.

Climate Change

As the world rotates around the sun, days are measured and as the Earth rotates on it's axis, hours are calculated. God placed the Earth in this perfect balance with the universe so that life may evolve and glorify His creation. In the beginning God created Adam and placed him in the garden to maintain.

Genesis 2:15 reads, "And the Lord God took the man, and put him into the Garden of Eden to dress it and to keep it."

Man was placed in the garden to care for it and to ensure it was in good health. Today, man is still responsible for maintaining God's creation and ensuring that the earth and the life that it supports is in good health.

As Christians we need to ensure our spiritual lives are in good health and in balance with God's commands to ensure His continued blessings and grace.

It is believed that 75% of the ice on the North Pole has disappeared in the last 40 years due to global warming. A number of different actions (e.g., clear cutting of the world's forests, burning of fossil fuels) by man has polluted the earth's atmosphere causing the oceans to warm, melting the world's glaciers and North Pole ice. This has resulted in weather patterns to change, storms to become more severe and caused more damage, an increase in the number of wild fires, and caused crops to fail and worldwide hunger.

Many of these disasters are self-inflicted by man due to the poor management of natural resources by countries around the world, the dumping of garbage in the rivers and oceans, and the burning of coal, oil, and natural gas. Man's greed and his complete disregard for his neighbor may place the earth on a path for total destruction.

The earth's atmosphere and the weather patterns that develop have no regard for boarders of countries. Consequently, the pollution that is pumped into the atmosphere by China may be the cause for the failure of crops in Russia, the flooding in Germany, and the prolonged drought in Africa.

Mankind is interconnected on this earth in many ways and is often affected by the sins committed by others. Examples of sins committed against mankind would include the poisoning the atmosphere, polluting the oceans, and killing the ocean's sea life, and traumatizing people with rumors of war.

We need to remember that the ultimate goal for Satan is to destroy the entire earth and all of mankind. He will use any means available to achieve this goal. He is extremely clever and is an expert at manipulating man by appealing to his ego and other frailties.

Genesis 2:16–17 reads, "And the Lord God commanded the man, saying, Of every tree of the garden thou mayest freely eat. But of the tree of the knowledge of good and evil, thou shalt not eat of it: for in the day that thou eatest thereof thou shalt surely die."

The earth, its gardens, and all of its natural beauty were created by God for man to enjoy and treasure. However, God also chose the Garden of Eden as a place for man to express love to God by following His commandments.

John 14:15 reads, "If you love me, keep my commandments."

If a Christian loves God he will keep God's commandments and statutes. However, no man has ever been able to keep all the commandments, except for Jesus Christ. And, it was the sacrifice of Jesus on the cross that paid the price for all of man's sin. Man's faith in Jesus Christ seals man's soul for eternal life.

Commandments

Romans 13:10 reads, "Love worketh no ill to his neighbor: therefore love is the filling of the law."

The Apostle Paul wrote that love is following the law. If we love God we will follow his commands and love our neighbor. The commandments that are found in Exodus 20 are an important part of Christianity. The law is a guide as to what God considers to be a sin. Every Christian should be able to recite the Ten Commandments from memory.

Today there are many who would like to eliminate the Ten Commandments and have them to be considered irrelevant. In fact, some are actually rewriting the Bible to fit their own personal life style.

The commandments that are found in Exodus 20 and Leviticus 19 are as follows:

1. You shall have no other Gods before me. Thou shall love thy neighbor as thyself.

2. You should not make any idols.

3. You shall not take the name of the Lord in vain.

4. Keep the Sabbath day holy.

5. Honor your father and your mother.

6. You shall not murder.

7. You shall not commit adultery.

8. You shall not steal.

9. You shall not bear false witness against your neighbor.

10. You shall not covet.

Matthew 22:37–39 reads, "Jesus said unto him, Thou shalt love the Lord thy God with all thy heart, and with all thy soul, and with all thy mind. This is the first and great commandment. And the second is like unto it. Thou shalt love thy neighbor as thyself."

The first commandment ensures that you place God as your first priority. No other person or thing should be considered to be more important in your daily life than praising and thanking God for His many blessings. The second command of loving your neighbor requires a loving attitude and heart, but careful not to be seen as one supporting or promoting sin.

Jesus Christ was the only person able to live on earth as a man and not sin. He spoke with sinners, ate with sinners, and He lead sinners to believe in Him as the Savior of the world. He did not accumulate a great deal of wealth, He did not assume a position of great authority or status in the government, and He did not build a mansion or accumulate great collections of jewelry or great herds of animals.

Jesus Christ did not join local social groups that were involved in promoting a new and popular pagan ritual. He used each and every encounter with sinners to teach the gospel. He healed many people of their different illnesses and asked them to believe in the gospel and God's plan for their life.

Kindness

As believers it is critical that we follow God's direction and allow his love, mercy and kindness to flow through us to those who are waiting for God's intervention. As believers our lives are all woven together as a fine tapestry working as one to form the master piece of God's creation.

God's word and commands in many cases are the complete opposite of what the world considers to be appropriate. One of the most repeated commands in the Bible is to love your neighbor. This one command in many cases is probably one of the most forgotten or ignored commands by the world. As believers we are representatives of God's message that He loved all people and gave His only Son that all who would believe would have eternal life. A believer has access to God's power, mercy and grace through prayer. Praying for a neighbor is in most cases the greatest gift or the most effective way of making a difference in a neighbor's life.

1 Samuel 16:7 reads, "But the Lord said unto Samuel, Look not on his countenance, or on height of his stature; because I have refused him: for the Lord seeth not as man seeth; for man looketh on the outward appearance, but the Lord looketh on the heart."

The world values a man by the number of his possessions, wealth, and his position within society. However, God through Samuel selected David to be the next King of Israel because of his heart. David was the youngest son of the family and worked as a shepherd for the family's sheep. But more importantly, God knew David's heart and knew He could mold David into a King that would further His kingdom. God values man by the condition of his heart and his kindness, mercy, and love that he shows to his neighbor.

Titus 3:4–5 reads, "But after that the kindness and love of God our Savior toward man appeared. Not by works of righteousness which we have done, but according to his mercy he saved us, by the washing of regeneratation, and renewing of the Holy Ghost."

Kindness is a gift from God to man for the purpose of allowing man to share this kindness with his neighbor. A believer is blessed beyond measure by the Holy Spirit who enters a man's life when he opens his heart and places his trust and faith in his Savior.

The emotional and impetuous Peter was an Apostle who had great love for his Lord and Savior.

The Apostle Peter understood the lifelong struggle of spiritual maturity that begins with faith that is based on the righteousness of God and our Savior Jesus the Christ. Faith opens the door to peace and spiritual knowledge. Spiritual knowledge allows for the understanding of God's truths with patience, self control, and without the world's corruption.

The Apostle Peter was also aware of those who were suffering and followed Jesus' example in showing mercy and kindness to those who were in need.

Acts 9:32–35 reads, "And it came to pass, as Peter passed throughout all quarters, he came down also to the saints which dwelt at Lydda. And there he found a certain man named Aeneas, which had kept his bed eight years, and was sick of the palsy. And Peter said unto him, Anneas, Jesus Christ maketh thee whole: arise, and make thy bed. And he arose immediately. And all that dwelt at Lydda and Saron saw him, and turned to the Lord."

Peter called upon the name of Jesus and allowed the power of His spirit to flow through him to heal Aeneas of the palsy. This act of kindness and mercy had a profound effect on Lydda and Saron and the entire community returned to worshiping the one true God.

Purification of the Soul

The Apostle Peter traveled to Joppa where he healed a woman named Tabitha (Dorcas).

Acts 9:40 reads, "But Peter put them all forth, and kneeled down, and prayed; and turning him to the body said, Tabitha, arise. And she opened her eyes, and when she saw Peter, she sat up."

Tabitha (Dorcas) was a woman full of good works and a believer. Peter's heart was touched by the generosity of this woman and those that testified of her many works of kindness. God saw that this woman had provided great service to the church. Peter prayed that she might continue so that others may receive the blessings of her service.

1 Peter 1:22 reads, "Seeing ye have purified your soul in obeying the truth through the Spirit unto unfeigned love of the brethren, see that ye love one another with a pure heart fervently."

The message is clear. If you want to know God it is essential that you love your neighbors and show them kindness. Jesus also stated that others would be able to identify you as a believer because of your kindness to your neighbor. This one principle is extremely important for a believer to grow and develop a relationship with their Lord and Savior. Other issues that will prevent or block communion with the Holy Spirit are sinfulness, greed, selfishness, and the lack of compassion for the poor and those in need.

Acts 5:15–16 reads, "Insomuch that they brought forth the sick into the streets, and laid them on beds and couches, that at the least the shadow of Peter passing by might overshadow some of them. There came also a multitude out of the cities round about unto Jerusalem, bringing sick folks, and them which were vexed with unclean spirits: and they were healed every one."

Mark 16:15–18 reads, "And he said unto them, Go ye into the world, and preach the gospel to every creature. He that believeth and is baptized shall be saved; but he that believeth not shall be dammed. And these signs shall follow them that believe; In my name shall they cast out devils; they shall speak with new tongues; They shall take up serpents; and if they drink any deadly thing, it shall not hurt them; they shall lay hands on the sick, and they shall recover."

The Apostle Peter was given the divine power of God to heal those who were suffering from sickness and to cast out demons from those who were possessed. The Apostle Peter with the divine power and mercy of the Holy Spirit blessed many and revealed God's kindness and love for His creation.

Compassion

THE APOSTLE JOHN WAS the youngest and lived the longest of the Apostles. The Apostle John's life was focused on being in the will of God and preaching the gospel of the kingdom of God and His return. He was beaten a number of times and spent time in prison for preaching the word of God.

John 7:38 reads, "He that believeth on me, as the scripture hath said, out of his belly shall flow rivers of living water."

The Apostle John had a profound relationship with Jesus and understood the importance of having the Holy Spirit direct his daily life. Jesus and the Holy Spirit transformed his personality, his values, and his heart to a man of great compassion and love for all of God's creation.

The Holy Spirit changed John the fisherman (the natural and fallen man) into a new man. The Apostle John was a man who lived for the purpose of saving souls and revealing God's plan for all of mankind. The Holy Spirit convicted John of his natural man's flaws and filled those areas with kindness and compassion for all those in need.

Jesus knew and trusted the Apostle John with the care of his mother (Mary). Jesus recognized the depth of kindness and love of the Apostle John and entrusted him as the provider for the care of Mary.

1 John 4:7–8 reads, "Beloved let us love one another: for love is of God; and every one that loveth is born of God, and knoweth God. He that loveth not knoweth not God; for God is love."

The Apostle John experienced the full meaning of love when he stood with Mary at the foot of the cross where Jesus the Christ gave his life for all. The love and kindness that is shared by each believer is the love and kindness from the Holy Spirit that indwells each believer.

The Apostle John was bold and direct in his writing and preaching in delivering the message of obeying God's commands and loving one another. This glorious Apostle continually spoke of God the Redeemer and the need to show charity for your neighbor. The Apostle John often explained that he who does not love his neighbor does not know God, for God is love. He would also speak of obeying God's commands and avoid all sin to prove your love for God.

1 John 4:20 reads, "If a man say, I love God, and hateth his brother, he is a liar: for he that loveth not his brother whom he hath seen, how can he love God whom he hath not see?"

Loving God is following His commands, glorifying and praising His name, and showing kindness to your neighbor. A believer's faith provides victory over the world and its values and allows the believer to grow in faith.

The Apostle John reminded man that to maintain a close relationship with God he must place his desires for the things of the world and his selfish desires in its proper perspective. You cannot love the world or the things of the world and also love God. You cannot have two masters; you will love one and hate the other.

Message of Self-Control

GOD'S TIMING, THE WHEN and how He works in our lives can be difficult to recognize and understand. However, there are times when our prayers are answered in such a powerful way that it can only be explained as the result of a miracle from God. We have a cause and effect relationship with God. When we are in His will and obedient to his word we receive blessings. When we are trusting in ourselves and disobedient to his word we experience the consequences. This relationship is subject to God's will and timing.

2 Peter 3:8 reads, "But, beloved, be not ignorant of this one thing, that one day is with the lord as a thousand years, and a thousand years as one day."

A believer has a personal relationship with his Lord and that relationship involves the continual exchange between the physical and the spiritual. God deals with each individual on an individual basis and is continually encouraging and strengthening each individual to fulfill His purpose of ministering to all of His creation.

God dealt with Moses directly, corrected him, encouraged him, and built him into a great leader that led over 600,000 people through the wilderness for 40 years. A number of individuals became angry in the Bible. However, becoming angry and losing self control or holding on to bitterness for an extended period of time can have a devastating effect on entire families, friends, and neighbors. Words spoken in anger or words spoken without compassion are words that are not forgotten and can cause permanent damage in any relationship. We need to be in prayer each day asking for God's grace, power, and mercy as we struggle to control our thoughts, emotions, and words. As we struggle with sin each day we have Jesus Christ as our example as a man who lived a life without sin.

As believers we need to be focused on the next assignment and getting prepared for the journey home. We also have the Holy Spirit that will comfort us when we are confused or in a difficult situation. We are complex individuals with many different challenges that only God can address and provide a solution.

Jesus Christ told the Apostle Peter that he would deny him three times. The Apostle Peter assured Jesus he would never deny him. However, the night when Jesus was arrested, beaten and taken for trial; Peter became extremely fearful and lost control of his emotions and denied that he knew Jesus three times. Peter was not prepared for the reality of the arrest and had slept rather then spent time in prayer and preparation as Jesus had requested.

1 Peter 5:8 reads, "Be sober, be vigilant; because your adversary the devil, as a roaring lion, walketh about, seeking whom he may devour:"

The Apostle Peter was proclaimed to be a courageous and committed follower of Jesus, however when reality hit, Peter's fear for his life took control and Satan was the victor. The importance of prayer is paramount in our battle with the world and Satan's demons. As Peter we are weak with many frailties and we need God's strength to carry us through the many challenges we face on a daily basis.

Mark 14: 54 reads, "And Peter followed him afar off, even into the palace of the high priest: and sat with the servants, and warmed himself at the fire."

As believers we have both successes and failures as we go through many experiences throughout our lives. We cannot be bystanders warming ourselves by the fire as Peter. We as believers are commissioned to follow God's plan for our lives.

Luke 22:31–32 reads, "And the Lord said, Simon, Simon, behold, Satan hath desired to have you, that he may sift you as wheat. But I have prayed for thee, that thy faith fail not: and when thou art converted, strengthen thy breather."

Jesus reminded Peter that Satan would like to destroy him and throw his ashes to the wind. Jesus also told Peter that he had prayed for him that his faith would be strong and he would continue to lead the Apostles.

God Changes Man

THE TRIALS WE EXPERIENCE throughout our lives are extremely valuable in molding our character and allowing us to relate to others going through those same experiences. The pain, the joy, and emotions that fill our life are an integral part of our spirit that gives us the sensitivity to appreciate and understand what others are feeling and thinking. The Holy Spirit will direct you to those people in need and will give you the words to say and in some cases tell you what part you need to accomplish.

1 John 1: 8–9 reads, "If we say that we have no sin, we deceive ourselves, and the truth is not in us. If we confess our sins, he is faithful and just to forgive us our sins, and to cleanse us from all unrighteousness."

As believers we are still natural man or fallen man. We still sin and in many cases we sin without our realizing it because of our limited understanding of God's purpose in our lives. Man's heart is desperately evil and has problems understanding the spiritual aspect of his life. As believers we are new creatures and the Holy Spirit now directs us and submits our prayers for God's blessings and strength. As believers we recognize sin and develop a sensitivity to sin and ask for forgiveness when we fail. We are still in a daily battle with Satan and his demons, and need to be in prayer asking for God's strength and wisdom in dealing with sin.

Ephesians 1:11–13 reads, "In whom also we have obtained an inheritance, being predestinated according to the purpose of him who worketh all things after the counsel of his own will: That we should be to the praise of his glory, who first trusted in Christ. In whom ye also trusted, after that ye heard the word of truth, the gospel of your salvation: in whom also after that ye believed, ye were sealed with that Holy Spirit of promise."

As believers we are sealed with the Holy Spirit and have the inheritance of eternal life. The Holy Spirit is the believers' advocate, protector, encourager, and acts as a guarantee of the inheritance for salvation. A believer with the assistance of the Holy Spirit continues the battle each day with sin. However, the Holy Spirit provides the believer with a greater sensitivity to sin and allows the believer the knowledge to avoid sin.

The Apostle John and the other Apostles matured greatly during the three years of ministry with Jesus and continued that maturity during their entire lives. The Apostle John lost self control when he asked Jesus to burn a Samaritan village to the ground for not welcoming Jesus on his travels through the village. Jesus rebuked the disciples and said he came to save man and not destroy man.

Luke 9:54–56 reads, "And when his disciples James and John saw this, they said, Lord, wilt thou that we command fire to come down from heaven, and consume them, even as Elijah did? But he turned, and rebuked them, and said, Ye know not what manner of spirit ye are of. For the Son of man is not come to destroy man's lives, but to save them. And they went to another village."

James and John (Sons of Thunder) were brothers who both became extremely angry and lost control of their emotions and wanted God to bring down fire from the heavens to destroy this Samaritan village.

Proverbs 14:29 reads, "He that is slow to wrath is of great understanding: but he that is hasty of spirit exalteth folly."

A person that is impatient and loses control of their temper will suffer the consequences in some way. As believers we struggle daily against principalities, against powers, and against wickedness. One of Satan's and his demon's priorities is to prevent you from accomplishing God's will for your life. God has a plan for your life and Satan will do everything he can do to prevent you from fulfilling that plan. If you find yourself consumed by anger you need take time before you respond and do or say something that you will later regret. It is important that we do not get distracted from God's plan for our lives and return to God's will as soon as possible.

Love Not the World

THE APOSTLE JOHN SPOKE of self control and the importance of not loving the things of the world. An idol is anything that consumes our time and energy and takes the place of God. Idols can be the love of possessions, money, recognition, and many more things that hold a greater value or a priority than the worship of God. A non-believer is enslaved to sin and the worship of idols, Satan and his demons. A person who is a believer has the Holy Spirit living in their life and has broken Satan's shackles.

1 John 2:15–17 reads, "Love not the world, neither the things that are in the world. If any man love the world, the love of the Father is not in him. For all that is in the world, the lust of the flesh, and the lust of the eyes, and the pride of life, is not of the Father, but is of the world. And the world passeth away, and the lust thereof: but he that doeth the will of God abideth for ever."

A person who loves Jesus Christ and follows God's commandments will break free of the sins of the world, its' idols and commune with the Holy Spirit. The Holy Spirit allows the believer to take control of his life and start to live a life that is focused on pleasing God and spending his time and energy helping others.

Psalm 119: 11–16 reads, "Thy word have I hid in mine heart, that I might not sin against thee. Blessed art thou, O Lord: teach me thy statutes. With my lips have I declared all the judgments of thy mouth. I have rejoiced in the way of thy testimonies, as much as in all riches. I will meditate in thy precepts, and have respect unto thy ways. I will delight myself in thy statutes: I will not forget thy word."

The believer is able to take on greater understanding and appreciation of God's word as he spends more time in meditation.

Message of the Law

THE MESSAGE OF THE law begins with God and his delivery of the law through Jesus, Moses and the prophets. Jesus told all of mankind that he had come to fulfill the law.

Matthew 5:17 reads, "Think not that I am come to destroy the law, or the prophets: I am not come to destroy, but to fulfill."

In Genesis God reveals His plan for both men and women.

Genesis 2:24 reads, "Therefore shall a men leave his father and his mother, and shall cleave unto his wife: and they shall be one flesh."

God created man and woman for a number of reasons. Their marriage is a sacred bond that is blessed by God for the purpose raising a family and instructing their children in God's teachings. This marriage of a man and woman is a union of mutual love, honor, respect and support. The Apostle Paul in his letter to the church of Thessalonica addressed some of the struggles found within the church.

1 Thessalonians 4:3–5 reads, "For this is the will of God, even your sanctification, that ye should abstain from fornication: That every one of you should know how to possess his vessel in sanctification and honor; Not in the lust of concupiscence, even as the Gentiles which know not God."

We are to control and prevent sin from contaminating our marriages or our bodies (vessels) that God has given us. The early church struggled with many issues found in a pagan society. Any monies related to these pagan practices were not allowed in God's holy church.

Deuteronomy 23:17–18 reads, "There shall be no whore of the daughters of Israel, nor a sodomite of the sons of Israel. Thou shalt not bring the hire of a whore, or the price of a dog, into the house of the Lord thy God for any vow: for even both these are abomination unto the Lord thy God."

Society was infested with many pagan practices that would attack and blame the Christians for any natural disaster that may occur. Christians were viewed as a threat by many persons who were benefiting financially from these pagan practices. No member of the local pagan society or any related funds were allowed into the house of the Lord.

God sent His angels to both Joseph and Mary to ensure this sacred bond of marriage would be complete and perfect under the law. The birth of Jesus created a sacred bond between God and man, and would allow Jesus to live a life as a man and take on the sins of all of mankind. Jesus took on the form of a man and lived as a man without sin to be the perfect sacrifice for all of man's sin. Jesus was both God and man and His life would bridge the gap between sin and heaven.

Society Today

SIN HAS EXISTED ON earth since the creation of man. Man was given free will to choose to love God and obey his commands or to worship sin and love Satan. At one point sin was so far out of control that God flooded the earth and destroyed all of mankind except for Noah and his family. However, man did continue to sin and suffered under the rule of many evil kings and pagan practices.

God recognized man's many failures and frailties and out of His pure grace offered His Only Son as a sacrifice for all of man's sin. The only possible way for man to enter heaven was for man to believe in Jesus Christ as his Savior and Lord.

Today we still see the ancient temples that were built around the world to worship evil gods and kings. Satan's purpose is to destroy man and all of God's blessings. One of his methods is to focus on man's weakness of pride and greed.

Satan is extremely clever and will use many different methods to destroy those that love God and keep his commandments. Satan today is using society and governments to pressure the church to accept pagan practices and not follow Biblical teachings. Some churches are actually rewriting the Bible and editing out major long lasting accepted biblical truths. Jesus said, "He did not come to abolish the Law but to fulfill it."

Exodus 20:1–17 reads, "And God spake all these words, saying. I am the Lord they God, which have brought thee out of the land of Egypt, out of the house of bondage. Thou shall have no other gods before me. Thou shalt not make unto thee any graven image, or any likeness of any thing that is in heaven above, or that is in the earth beneath, or that is in the water under the earth. Thou shalt not bow down thyself to them, nor serve them: for I the Lord thy God am a jealous God, visiting the iniquity of the fathers upon the children unto the third and fourth generation of them that hate me; And showing mercy unto thousands of them that love me, and keep my commandments. Thou shalt not take the name of the Lord thy God in vain: for the Lord will not hold him guiltless that taketh his name in vain. Remember the Sabbath day, to keep it holy. Six days shalt thou labor, and do all thy work: But the seventh day is the Sabbath of the Lord thy God: in it thou shalt not do any work, thou, nor thy son, nor thy daughter, thy manservant, nor thy maidservant, nor thy cattle, nor thy stranger that is within thy gates. For in six days the Lord made heaven and earth, the sea, and all that in them is, and rested the seventh day, wherefore the Lord blessed the sabbath day, and hallowed it. Honor thy father and thy mother: that thy days maybe long upon the land which the Lord thy God giveth thee. Thou shalt not kill. Thou shalt not commit adultery. Thou shalt not steal. Thou shalt not bear false witness against the neighbor. Thou shalt not covet thy neighbor's house, thou shalt not covet thy neighbor's wife, nor his manservant, nor his maidservant, nor his ox, nor his ass, nor any thing that is thy neighbor's."

These commandments begin with loving the Lord your God with all your heart, soul, and mind. God should hold the most important position in your life and be your first priority in any decision. Our very existence on this planet is only possible with God's grace and love. We are commanded not to bow down or serve any other God. Another god would be anything you consider to be more important than worshiping God.

The laws of today reflect and follow the values of today's society. The laws and values of today continue to change with the issue and it's popularity and as groups of people organize to communicate a common message. For example, spitting on the sidewalk was an important issue at one time and in response many detailed laws were written with fines to discourage that practice. This law has fallen out of popularity and is normally not enforced even at professional baseball games.

God's laws and commands have and will never change.

Adultery Today

Thou shalt not commit adultery is a commandment that is an extremely serious sin that has been responsible for countless numbers of marriages ending over countless years. Adultery is a sin that occurs within a marriage between a man and woman. Adultery is committed when a man or a woman is unfaithful to the sacred marriage bond. The reason why this sin is so common today is because of lack of moral standards and in some cases the actual promotion of pagan practices too perverse to describe.

Stealing of goods and property is a common sin today that occurs throughout the world. Stealing would include corruption and other methods to defraud or cheat people out of the money or property. In some countries today, corruption is so prevalent that laws are seldom enforced by local authorities. There are some groups that believe they are entitled to whatever they wish. These individuals will actually kill another individual if they possess something they wish. King David was guilty of this sin and many others.

To bear false witness against your neighbor is to tell a lie. Man has a fallen nature and will lie for any number of different reasons in many different situations. Many have been convinced by the evil one (the great liar) that lying is not a sin. Lying is a very powerful tool that can bring great harm to any person in many different ways. Lying is so prevalent today that it is very difficult to determine the truth from a lie.

Exodus 23:1–3 reads, "Thou shalt not raise a false report: put not thine hand with the wicked to be an unrighteous witness. Thou shalt not follow a multitude to do evil: neither shalt thou speak in a cause to decline after many to wrest judgment. Neither shalt thou countenance a poor man in his cause."

As Christians we need to realize Satan is the great liar and is working feverously to destroy as many lives as possible. God commanded man to love God with all his heart, soul and mind. God also commanded man to love his neighbor as himself. King David loved his son Solomon and directed him to keep all of God's commandments and statutes to ensure he would have good success.

1 Kings 2:3 reads, "And keep the charge of the Lord thy God, to walk in his ways, to keep his statutes, and his commandments, and his judgments, and his testimonies, as it is written in the law of Moses, that thou mayest prosper in all that thou doest, and whithersoever thou turnest thyself."

Jesus told all of mankind that if they loved Him they needed to obey His commandments and statutes.

John 14:15–16 reads, "If ye love me, keep my commandents. And I will pray the Father, and he shall give you another Comforter, that he may abide with you for ever."

In addition to the commandments God has provided many rules and statutes that a believers needs to follow and apply to their daily lives. When the scribe asked Jesus what was the greatest commandment, Jesus answered with the beginning of the Ten Commandments. Deuteronomy 6:4–5 reads, "Hear, O Israel: The Lord our God is one Lord: And thou shalt love the Lord thy God with all thine heart, and with all thy soul, and with all thy might." Jesus also included a command from Leviticus 19:13 that reads, "Thou shalt not avenge, nor bear any grudge against the children of thy people, but thou shalt love thy neighbor as thyself: I am the Lord."

Jesus used these verses from the law to answer the scribe's question as to what is the most important command. Both of these verses are based on love for God and love for your neighbor. All of our decisions and opinions should be based first on love.

A New Creature

A new believer takes on a new character and must identify and repent of their sins. A new believer is convicted by the Holy Spirit of the sin in their lives and must bury the old desires, values, and temptations. There is nothing impossible for God to accomplish in a person's life.

Ephesians 4:29–30 reads, "Let no corrupt communication proceed out of your mouth, but that which is good to the use of edifying, that it may minister grace unto the hearers. And grieve not the Holy Spirit of God, whereby ye are sealed unto the day of redemption."

We need to be careful about the words we use on a daily basis. Do we speak out of love and concern for our neighbor's well-being? Is our language guided by the Holy Spirit? We need to run from evil and not be swallowed up by evil pressures and temptations. Today's society and its values are full of evil and those that are trying to convince man that there is nothing wrong with today's morals.

Justice for mankind is based on truth. Christians should not be involved in or in some way associated with persons or organizations that use lies or false reports to discredit people.

Hebrew 10:23–25 reads, "Let us hold fast the profession of our faith without wavering; for he is faithful that promised; And let us consider one another to provoke unto love and to good works; Not forsaking the assembling of ourselves together, as the manner of some is; but exhorting one another: and so much the more, as ye see the day approaching."

As Christians we hold fast to God's promise of eternal life. We realize that it is only God's grace that allows us to place our faith in God's only Son as your Savior and Lord. Jesus Christ was the only person that lived a perfect life without sin. It was the sacrifice of this perfect life that washed away all of man's sin.

God is a loving God that wants all people to spend eternity with Him and to experience all of His grace, mercy, and blessings. However, to experience God's grace, mercy, and blessings for eternity one must place God first in their life and place all of their trust and faith in Him. The believers that have crossed over or will cross over the bridge built on the death of God's only Son, Jesus Christ will experience blessings too numerous to count and will be able to rejoice as they never have rejoiced before.

God is able to look into the heart of a person and determine if that person will grow in faith and be obedient to God's word. These are men and women that have grown in great humility and have fallen at God's feet in worship. God looked at these men and women not for who they are or were, but for what they would become.

God created each person as a unique individual with a unique purpose in life. Some are able to identify God's purpose for their life in a short amount of time and others struggle to find that purpose for many years. God's plan for mankind is a perfect plan and uses each person's talents and gifts at the appropriate time.

Conclusion

As believers we are all transformed from being a self-centered individual to a person that places Jesus Christ as our center. We grow in maturity as we become more obedient and are challenged to accept more responsibilities. Our relationship with God evolves as He sees we are trustworthy and able to accomplish spiritual tasks.

God's messengers have always delivered a message that becoming a Christian is a lifelong process of living as a servant to others with the leading and strength of the Holy Spirit.

Romans 12:1–3 reads, "I beseech you therefore, brethren, by the mercies of God, that ye present your bodies a living sacrifice, holy, acceptable unto God, which is your reasonable service. And be not conformed to this world: but be ye transformed by the renewing of your mind, that ye may prove what is that good, and acceptable, and perfect, will of God. For I say, through the grace given unto you, to every man that is among you, not to think of himself more highly then he ought to think; but to think soberly, according as God hath dealt to every man the measure of faith."

We all need to take an honest evaluation of the message we are sending to our loved ones and our neighbors. It is also important to realize that evil has a great deal of influence over what we hear and see on a daily basis. If at all possible we need to avoid evil and not to be entrapped into some never ending debate over good and evil. We rest in God's inerrant word the Bible and place all of our understanding in God's love and grace. We are all sinners and are subject to our fallen nature. We are at war with evil each day and we live in faith under the protection of our Lord and Savior.

Today we see the results of a society that has failed to provide or follow basic moral values. We see generation after generation of children left alone to wander the streets without any parental guidance. Many of these children drop out of school at early age and begin a life of crime in order to survive. To stop this vicious cycle of crime and violence society needs to make some major changes. Children that are at risk need to be indentified at an early age and closely mentored until such time they are productive members of society. This is one area that has been ignored for many years due to many different reasons. Both state and federal agencies with limited funding has struggled for years to meet this critical need. This situation is now out of control to where young children are involved in serious crimes daily in most cities.

Christians, the church, and the family are under attack from Satan and his demons from every direction. Children are being attacked at their schools and being forced to read and learn about pagan practices. Schools are teaching children that there is no God, no creator, and no divine plan and purpose for their lives. Satan and his demons are using every possible method to undermine and discredit the family. Divorce is an easy and common solution used today to resolve any disagreement in a marriage. The result is millions of children are left without the love and support of a father and mother. Satan and his demons are attacking the church in many different ways. The church for years has not been taxed due to it's work of providing food and shelter for the poor for the world. Now governments are threatening to disallow this tax emption if churches do not comply with new government laws, rules and regulations.

God loves us and is always available to hear our concerns and wishes. God communicates with us in a number of different ways. He may use the Holy Spirit to guide us, angels to lead us, dreams to instruct us, nature to reveal His beauty and power, a pillar of fire to direct us, Jesus to comfort us, and prophets and the Bible for revelation.

God spoke to Adam and Eve in the garden.

Genesis 3:8 reads, "And they heard the voice of the Lord God walking in the garden in the cool of the day: and Adam and his wife hid themselves from the presence of the Lord God amongst the trees of the garden. And the Lord God called unto Adam, and said unto him, Where are thou?"

God loved Adam and Eve and called out to them with concern. Even though Adam and Eve sinned God still clothed them. God is always there searching for us even when we are lost deep in sin. His love is never ending.

Jesus instructed us to seek first the kingdom of God.

Matthew 6:33 reads, "But seek ye first the kingdom of God, and his righteousness; and all these things shall be added unto you."

Jesus' message to mankind is clear; we are instructed to continually seek after God's kingdom and His righteousness. As Christians our first priority is to worship God and to trust God for any material needs. God will provide for us and we are instructed not to worry about tomorrow.

The Holy Spirit was sent by Jesus to provide a message of peace and comfort. The Holy Spirit communicates continually to the Christian each day and in many different ways.

John 14:26–27 reads, "But the Comforter, which is the Holy Ghost, whom the Father will send in my name, he shall teach you all things, and bring all things to your remembrance, whatsoever I have said unto you. Peace I leave with you, my peace I give unto you: not as the world giveth, give I unto you. Let not your heart be troubled, neither let it be afraid."

The Christian has a very unique and wonderful relationship with the Holy Spirit. The Holy Spirit is extremely powerful and is able to bring great peace and comfort to the Christian. The God that raised Jesus from the dead is the same God and Holy Spirit that lives within the Christian today. (Romans 8:11)

Bibliography

Brenton, Lancelot C. *The Septuagint with Apocrypha: Greek and English*. Peabody, MA: Hendrickson, 1986.

Bruce, Alexander Balmain. *The Training of the Twelve*. Keats Publishing, 1979.

Bruner, Frederick Dale. *Matthew: A Commentary*. Cambridge, UK: Eerdmans, 2004.

Buswell, James Oliver Jr. *Problems in the Prayer Life: From a Pastor's Question Box*. Chicago: The Bible Institute, 1928.

Edersheim, Rev. D. *Sketches of Jewish Social Life in the Day of Christ*. Hodder and Stoughton, 1989.

Geikie, Cunningham. *The Life and Words of Christ*. New York: Appleton and Company, 1879.

Lawrence, Brother. *The Practice of the Presence of God and Spiritual Maxims*. Benton Press, 2013.

Lewis, C. S. *Miracles*. New York: HarperOne, 2000.

Ryle, J. C. *Holiness*. Renaissance Classics, 2012.

Spurgeon, Charles H. *Spurgeon's Sermon Notes: Over 250 Sermons Including Notes, Commentary and Illustrations*. Edited by David Otis Fuller. Grand Rapids: Mt. Kregel, 1990.

Webster, Douglas D. *Finding Spiritual Direction*. Downers Grove: InterVarsity, 1991.